Amanda —
Mau
Weekends be
Magical —
Love
Annie
XXX

$3.99
①
22

# The
# Country Weekend
## Cookbook

# The
# Country Weekend
# Cookbook

## ANTOINETTE PARKES

*Foreword by Margaret Lane*

*Drawings by John Bigg*

**COLLINS**
St James's Place, London
1981

William Collins Sons & Co. Ltd
London · Glasgow · Sydney · Auckland
Toronto · Johannesburg

BRITISH LIBRARY CATALOGUING IN PUBLICATION DATA

Parkes, Antoinette
The Country Weekend Cookbook
1. Cookery
I. Title
641.5   TX717

ISBN 0 00 216525 2

First published 1981
© Antoinette Parkes 1981

*Phototypeset in Baskerville
by Western Printing Services Ltd, Bristol*

*Printed in Great Britain by
Butler & Tanner Ltd
Frome and London*

*For Harry and Sam*

# Contents

# FOREWORD

It seems to me that domestic cooking in this country has noticeably improved since the disappearance of the living-in cook. Nowadays we have had to learn to do the job our-selves, and this, in many cases, has led to the discovery that cooking is a fascinating business. All sorts of new or foreign ideas are worth exploring, experiments are made in private with the family, and entertaining three or four friends for a weekend takes on the excitement and satisfaction of a performance.

Of course it is time-consuming and has its frustrations and anxieties, but what worthwhile enterprise has not? Nowadays we come to our friends' tables with a new interest, ready to swap ideas and recipes and to take a lively interest in every dish. A good host or hostess today means a good cook, and I admit I am lucky in knowing quite a few of them.

The first trick one has to learn is to be organized, so that a hospitable weekend doesn't have to mean slavery in the kitchen for one person while the rest enjoy themselves elsewhere, or—worse still—invade the working area with cries of 'Can I help?' and then lean against the sink to smoke and talk.

Menus must be worked out and shopping done a day or two ahead. The preliminary stages of various dishes can be safely got through and stacked in the refrigerator. Pastry, I have always found, improves with a day or two in the deep-freeze. Flan cases can be made ahead and stowed away, so can a 'bank' of good stock (the residues of chicken carcases and lobster shells), and pre-cooked purées of gooseberries and blackcurrants.

We owe a lot, of course, to the modern technology of the kitchen. The deep-freeze helps to solve the problem of supply, especially in the country, where good shops can be a long way off. And the 'food processors' of different sorts have taken a lot of drudgery out of the kitchen. I don't, myself, possess the elaborate kinds, since I am addicted to my old set of good French knives and an ancient chopping-board, but I could no longer face cooking without my electric mixing-bowl and liquidizer. The one has taken both time and arm-aching out of cakes and puddings, the other makes child's play of soups and sauces. The mess and tedium of beating something for an hour (as in the old cookery books), or rubbing things through sieves, has gone for ever.

In spite of my gratitude for these modern inventions, however, I must confess to a fascination with simple and traditional methods, due perhaps to my preference for uncomplicated rather than rich and elaborate dishes. But simple and traditional methods, however romantic, have their disadvantages, which in our cosseted modern age we are unwilling to put up with. There was a time, when I lived in a small thatched Hampshire farmhouse, when I became obsessed with spit-roasting and cooked many a slowly turning chicken or turkey before an open fire. The result was always delicious, but the disadvantage was that, even with a metal fire-screen and a three-foot basting-spoon, the cook was roasted sooner than the bird, and the open fire had to be kept so hot that hungry guests were apt to faint at table.

Another period of romantically primitive cooking was in Connemara, where one lives with a turf fire, and the 'pot oven' and hanging kettle are traditional equipment. The pot-oven is a heavy lidded iron pot on three legs, in which everything can be cooked, since it stands in a mound of hot ash with nuggets of red-hot peat constantly piled on the rimmed lid. This was the way to make one's daily loaf of soda bread (eaten warm—heavens, how delicious!) and I even proved its efficacy on one occasion by baking croissants in it. But the pot-oven's capacity is no more than a large saucepan's, and the fine turf-ash smothers everything, including oneself, so that in the end one comes back to the gas or electric oven with humble gratitude.

One final piece of primitive know-how goes back to the times I spent in an old house in Morocco and learned to cook meat on skewers over charcoal in the manner familiar to everyone nowadays under the name of barbecue. The snag in *that* method is that the smoke is so frightful that the cooking must be done out of doors, which in the *kasbah* means the narrow alley outside your house, or on the flat roof a long way from your kitchen. All very exotic and medieval, of course, but uncongenial to anyone who has strong feelings about privacy and dislikes being stared at or trodden on while cooking.

Which brings one back to the technical comforts of the modern kitchen, and the dodges available—freezers and dish-washers and the like—which make the cooking for a companionable weekend not only possible but pleasurable. The other weekends in Antoinette Parkes's collection may well be more sophisticated than mine, but that can't be helped. I tend to be a little old-fashioned, roasting apples or snipe before an open fire in a little 'Dutch oven' and preferring the flavour of toast eaten straight from a toasting-fork rather than a pop-up toaster. But then, what are these weekends for, after all? Each guest, one hopes, is

> *Seeking the food he eats,*
> *And pleas'd with what he gets . . .*

Margaret Lane

# INTRODUCTION

The majority of entertaining in the country centres around the weekend, and to my mind the nicest way of seeing friends is to have them to stay. Good food and a relaxed atmosphere are essential. To stay with someone who makes you feel a burden is as unpleasant as it must be for them to have you. I have been waiting for years for someone to write a book on how to produce delicious food that can be prepared either in advance, or very simply at the last moment so that you can actually see your friends without at the end of the weekend being exhausted by the effort. Finally I decided to put the book together myself.

I have had enormous fun testing these recipes. Until I started I had avoided cooking whenever possible and would always rather be doing something else. But I have now discovered that half the effort of being a cook is in planning the menus, and when that chore has been removed the actual cooking is simple. Another pleasure has been that, whereas most of us tend to cook in a certain style, so that each of our meals seems to taste similar, trying out everybody else's menus has broken down that particular habit for me.

I have concentrated on meals that can be cooked in advance. It is astonishing how much preparation can usefully be done beforehand. None of these recipes takes enormous skill, some do require time, but others are startlingly simple. Any reasonably competent cook could tackle any of the dishes here, and there are menus suitable for the complete novice. I have tried to arrange the menus with a Friday supper that won't spoil if the visitors are late; a light lunch on Saturday (don't overwhelm your guests with quantity); and a rather special Saturday dinner, as I have assumed that extra friends may appear for this meal. Then a traditional lunch on Sunday. Finally, I have included Sunday supper, since although your guests will probably have left by then, you and your family will need to eat something. This meal is extremely simple and usually makes use of leftovers.

The recipes are generally for six people with the exception of Saturday dinner for eight and Sunday supper for two. I have indicated which recipes can be made 'in advance', which usually means the day before; and where only part of the dish can be prepared beforehand, the stopping point is indicated with an asterisk. I have also noted the time needed for preparation, and sometimes for cooking, so that the particularly reluctant or busy cook can easily choose the most suitable recipe for her (or his) needs.

Antoinette Parkes

# ACKNOWLEDGEMENTS

I would like to thank Betty Holdaway and Pat Laughlin for typing the manuscript; Rosie Collins, without whose encouragement I would never have dared start the book; all the contributors; Hilary Davies of Collins; and lastly my husband David, who has helped me throughout.

*Built at the turn of the century,
Blackbridge House is hidden away above
the upper reaches of the Beaulieu river.*

# JANUARY

—◆—

## Margaret Lane

Margaret Lane's house is like an Aladdin's cave – every corner and table filled with something I covet. The kitchen is small and above the electric cooker is a beautifully painted hornet's nest complete with hornets, and a vine surrounds the round window, all painted by Margaret's husband. The dining room (which wisely holds no more than eight) is separated from the kitchen by an exquisite Victorian scrap screen.

'Although we have a good village shop,' says Margaret, 'we live some miles from a small town, so I keep a pretty full deep-freeze – home-made bread, fish and fruit, windfall apples, peeled and sliced, that sort of thing, and sometimes pre-cooked food. I keep a big herb bed with fennel, sage, rosemary, tarragon and about eight varieties of mint. I don't have much time for gardening, so do not have a vegetable patch.

'I lead a fairly routine working life, disappearing into my study for the morning and usually out of doors in the afternoon. I try to work again between five and seven. I like to plan in advance, and don't like spending endless hours in the kitchen, where I prefer to be alone. I find it distracting to have other people around, and as for having young children . . .!'

Weekend guests at Blackbridge are treated to the luxury (or discipline) of breakfast in bed, following the sensible dictum of the philosopher Jeremy Bentham: 'Breakfast my guests, whoever they are, have in their rooms, and at their own hour, and by themselves. . .' For this purpose a special book is kept, with the breakfast menu each person prefers. The advantage (for the cook) of this comfortable arrangement is that she can get on with her kitchen chores in solitude and peace while her guests are upstairs munching croissants and reading the Sunday papers.

Margaret makes her own wholemeal bread and wine vinegars. As she says, 'It's expensive to buy the latter, and if you have a house where wine is regularly drunk, it is easy to make; you can have lots of different herb-flavoured ones in different bottles, made from dregs of wine by a 'vinegar mother'.

'I can't bear waste. I serve my vinaigrette separately from salads, as I hate to throw away a beautifully dressed Webb lettuce, not to mention tomatoes and cucumbers. I make all my own pastry by hand, using generally rough puff, which is perfect for almost everything. Occasionally I buy puff pastry if I am busy, but I don't like machine-made pastry.'

The food, like everything else at Blackbridge, is simple, but interesting.

## Friday

**SUPPER**

Bortsch without Meat

Cold Stuffed Sea Trout
Rice Salad
Green Salad

Apple and Almond Delight
Cream

## Saturday

**LUNCH**

Haddock, Bacon and Mushroom Quiche
Mixed Salad
Apple Salad
'My' Salad Dressing

Cheeseboard with Oatcakes and Brown Toast
Fruit

**DINNER**

Huntingdon Eggs

Chicken Maryland
Fried Bananas
Sweetcorn
Green Salad

Tangier Orange
Tuiles d'Amandes
Cream

## Sunday

**LUNCH**

Chicken Livers en Brochette
Brown Rice
Green Salad

Bonita
Sponge Fingers

**SUPPER**

Sea Trout Kedgeree
Green Salad

Oatcakes
Cheese and Fruit

# Friday Supper

## (for 6 people)

### HUNTINGDON SPECIAL

Before supper, gathered round a good fire, I find most people enjoy what has come to be known as a Huntingdon Special, i.e. a measure of whisky on ice, with a dash of ginger wine, and the glass filled up with unsweetened grapefruit juice. Stir well.

When friends are arriving on a Friday evening I do not want to be in the kitchen at all, so usually devise a meal that can be prepared earlier in the day.

### BORTSCH WITHOUT MEAT

*4 large beets*
*1 onion*
*Large clove garlic*
*Salt and pepper*
*2 eggs*
$1\frac{3}{4}$ litres   *$1\frac{1}{2}$ quarts water*
*1 cup tomato purée*
*1 tablespoon lemon juice*
*A little sugar*
*Sour cream*

Peel and cut up the beets, crush the garlic, chop the onion and bring all to the boil in water in a large saucepan. Simmer gently for 45 minutes.

Add 1 cup of tomato purée (or a small tin of tomatoes), a tablespoon of fresh lemon juice, salt and pepper to taste and a little sugar. Cook until the vegetables are tender, then purée in a liquidizer and return to the pan.

Beat 2 eggs well, add a little of the hot soup and stir into the pan before serving. Serve in warmed soup bowls, pouring a ring of sour cream on the surface of each.

### COLD STUFFED SEA TROUT

$1\frac{1}{2}$–$1\frac{3}{4}$ kg   *A 3–4 lb sea trout*
*A salmon's head or steak*
*Juice of 1 lemon*
*Salt and pepper*
*A little oil*
*To garnish: lemon and*
    *cucumber slices,*
    *2 lettuce hearts and a*
    *bunch of watercress*

Sprinkle lemon juice inside the fish, season with salt and pepper. Oil the whole skin lightly and wrap in foil, with the extra salmon head or steak. Put in the oven at 350°F 180°C gas 4, cooking for 40–45 minutes *in all*. Unwrap and allow to cool.

# Friday Supper
## continued

STUFFING

1 lemon
A handful of chopped parsley
125 g    4 oz butter
Salt, pepper, garlic salt
A little mayonnaise (see
page 116)

Pound the extra fish meat with the juice and grated rind of the lemon, a handful of chopped parsley, butter, seasoning and a little mayonnaise. The stuffing should be fairly firm: if it seems too moist a small handful of fine white breadcrumbs may be added.

Remove the skin from the top of the fish, then loosen and lift this from the bone and lay it, cut side uppermost, on a serving dish. Spread evenly with the stuffing. Remove all the bones from the remaining half of the fish and reverse it carefully on to the stuffing. Skin this half.*

Garnish with sliced lemon and cucumber down the middle and surround with lettuce hearts and watercress.

*This much can be prepared a day in advance.

RICE SALAD

225 g    8 oz Patna rice
3 tablespoons mayonnaise (see
page 116)
Salt and pepper
1 small onion, chopped
225 g    8 oz packet of frozen mixed
vegetables

Pour the rice into boiling salted water and simmer until tender but firm (about 12 minutes). Drain, rinse well with cold water and spread out to dry on a tray covered with foil.

Cook the mixed vegetables, drain and stir in the mayonnaise. Combine with the rice and add the finely chopped onion. Test the seasoning. Serve cold, piled up in a shallow dish, accompanied by a crisp green salad.

## APPLE AND ALMOND DELIGHT

1¼ kg    3 lb cooking apples
75 g    3 oz ground almonds
75 g    3 oz butter
75 g    3 oz white sugar
½ teacup of cider
2 tablespoons honey
1 egg
Flaked almonds
1 teacupful of white
breadcrumbs
Thin peel of a lemon
Cream

Peel, core and quarter the apples. Stew to a pulp with the cider and allow to cool. Stir in the honey, then the breadcrumbs and finely chopped lemon peel. Spread in a baking dish.

Beat the butter and sugar to a cream, add the ground almonds and beaten egg. Spread this smoothly over the apple, strew with flaked almonds and bake at 350°F 180°C gas 4 until golden brown.

Good hot or cold. Serve with cream.

# Saturday Lunch

(for 6 people)

## HADDOCK, BACON AND MUSHROOM QUICHE

| | |
|---|---|
| 450 g | *1 lb smoked haddock* |
| 150 ml | *4–5 fluid oz milk* |
| | *2 eggs* |
| 25 g | *1 oz grated Cheddar cheese* |
| | *3 thin rashers streaky bacon* |
| 125 g | *4 oz button mushrooms, sliced* |
| | *2 tablespoons double cream* |
| | *Short crust or rough puff pastry* |
| | *Pepper, ground mace* |

Make the pastry and chill for 15 minutes (see below). Roll out and line a 9-inch (22-cm) flan ring: put in the refrigerator and set the oven at 375°F 190°C gas 5.

Cover the fish with milk, bring slowly to the boil and simmer gently until tender (about 10 minutes). Take out the fish, reserving the milk, remove any skin and bones, flake the flesh.

Remove the rind from the bacon and grill until crisp, then cut it up with scissors. Beat the eggs, add the grated cheese and the milk, the sliced mushrooms, bacon and haddock. Season with pepper, but taste the mixture before adding any salt – it may not need it. Add the double cream.*

Spoon the mixture into the pastry-lined flan ring and sprinkle all over with mace. Bake in pre-set oven until the filling is set and slightly risen and the top golden brown – about 25 minutes.

*This much can be prepared in advance.

### ROUGH PUFF PASTRY

| | |
|---|---|
| 225 g | *8 oz plain flour* |
| 125 g | *4 oz firm margarine* |
| 50 g | *2 oz lard* |
| | *¼ teaspoon salt* |
| 150 ml | *¼ pint very cold water* |

My rough puff pastry is perhaps not quite conventional, but it works. It must be prepared a day in advance.

Sift the flour and salt into a bowl, cut up the lard and rub it into the flour. Mix with water to a firm dough and refrigerate for about 15 minutes.

Roll out the dough into a rectangular shape, cut the (cold) margarine into flat pieces and place them over two-thirds of the pastry. Fold over the empty flap, fold again, turn the pastry round, press the open ends with a rolling pin and roll out as before. Fold again and refrigerate for half an hour. (Freezer compartment works faster.)

Repeat this process three times. I do not know why but deep freezing overnight and unfreezing in the refrigerator before using always seems to improve both puff and rough puff pastry.

Serve the quiche with an apple salad – peeled, cored and diced eating apples, mixed with finely chopped onion and salad dressing, and sprinkled with chopped parsley – and a mixed salad – lettuce, cress, cucumber, tomato etc. – accompanied by what I call 'my' salad dressing, which I always serve separately.

'MY' SALAD DRESSING
(makes 2 pints/1 litre)

*1 large egg or 2 small*
*Scant teaspoon salt*
*¼ teaspoon pepper*
*Scant teaspoon sugar*
*½ teaspoon powdered mustard*
*Large peeled clove garlic*
75 ml  *½ teacup white wine vinegar*
575 ml  *1 pint olive or*
*sunflower oil*
*Water*

Break the egg into the liquidizer, add salt, pepper, garlic, sugar and mustard. Turn on and blend. Add vinegar and continue blending, then add the oil in a very thin stream until it thickens. When the mixture appears to have become almost solid, add water in a thin trickle – still blending – to bring the amount up to 1½ pints (850 ml) of dressing. Funnel it into screw-top bottles and use as required.

This will keep for two to three weeks in a cool place.

## OATCAKES

To make 6 (24 quarters):

500 g  *1 lb medium oatmeal*
175 g  *6 oz fine oatmeal*
*½ teaspoon salt*
*½ teaspoon bicarbonate*
*of soda*
50 g  *2 oz good dripping*

Making oatcakes is a slow business, but home-made ones are so incomparably better than shop varieties that it is worth making a batch during the week for a special occasion.

Mix the dry ingredients: put the dripping in the centre, pour on about ½ pt (257 ml) hot water to soften it, and mix. Make up a fairly moist dough. Take a handful, knead it into a round on a board scattered with fine oatmeal, press out gently with your knuckles and pinch round the edge until you have a good smooth round shape. Dust a rolling-pin with fine meal and roll out gently to ⅛″ (4 mm) thickness, about 8″ (20 cm) in diameter.

Cut the round into quarters, slip them on to a hot griddle or heavy iron frying pan and cook until the edges curl slightly and the underneath is faintly coloured. Finish by toasting in a moderate oven, 350°F 180°C gas 4, or under a *very* gentle grill. Dry off for an hour in a cool oven or near the fire and keep in an air tight tin.

# Saturday Dinner

## (for 8 people)

### HUNTINGDON EGGS

9 eggs (1 per person and 1 over)  
150 ml  ¼ pint mayonnaise (see page 116)  
150 ml  ¼ pint double cream  
12½ g  ½ oz leaf gelatine  
275 ml  10½ oz tin of beef consommé  
Clove of garlic  
Parsley

Put eight cocottes in the refrigerator. Coddle the eggs until hard. Cool, shell and chop them coarsely. Whip the cream, mix with the mayonnaise and crushed garlic, fold in the chopped eggs and chill in the refrigerator.

Soak the gelatine in water, and when soft stir into the heated consommé until dissolved. Cool.

Divide the egg mixture between the cocottes, smoothing the surface with a teaspoon. Return to the refrigerator until really cold (or the freezer compartment for a few minutes). By this time the consommé jelly should be cool but still liquid. Spoon a little all over the surface of the egg in each cocotte and return to the refrigerator until set – about 5 minutes. Once this thin film of jelly is firm, the rest of the consommé can safely be spooned on without fear of clouding. Return to the refrigerator.*

Decorate each cocotte with a tiny tuft of parsley and serve with thin brown bread and butter.

*This much can be prepared a day in advance.

### CHICKEN MARYLAND

8 fresh chicken pieces  
1 beaten egg  
White flour  
Fine white breadcrumbs  
125 g  4 oz unsalted butter  
4 bananas  
225 g  8 oz sweetcorn, tinned or frozen  
Salt and pepper

Season the chicken pieces with salt and pepper, dust all over with flour, then coat with beaten egg and finally breadcrumbs. Sauté the pieces in clarified butter in a large pan or place in the oven for about half an hour at 350°F 180°C gas 4, basting occasionally. They should be cooked slowly, or they will brown before they are cooked through. Drain on a paper towel and keep hot.

Peel the bananas and halve them cross-wise, dust with flour, coat with beaten egg and roll in breadcrumbs. Fry in butter until soft; drain and keep hot.

The sweetcorn meanwhile should be simmered in salted water until tender. Drain, then stir in a good knob of butter.

Arrange chicken and bananas on a silver dish; serve sweetcorn separately, accompanied by a good green salad.

# *Saturday Dinner*

## continued

### TANGIER ORANGE

*Thin-skinned juicy oranges*
*6 tablespoons soft*
  *brown sugar*
*2 teaspoons powdered*
  *cinnamon*
*Whipped cream*
*Toasted almonds*

Allow 1 large or 2 small oranges per person and one or two over for juice. Slice the whole oranges thinly and lay in a thick shallow pan. Add orange juice, brown sugar and cinnamon. Cover and simmer until tender, about 10 minutes. Cool, then refrigerate for several hours or overnight. Transfer carefully with a fish slice on to a china dish* and top with dollops of whipped cream and lightly toasted almonds. Serve with Tuiles d'Amandes.

*This much can be prepared a day in advance.

### TUILES d'AMANDES

|         | *2 egg whites* |
| 125 g | *4 oz castor sugar* |
| 50 g | *2 oz flour* |
|         | *½ teaspoon vanilla essence* |
| 25 g | *1 oz blanched shredded*
  *almonds* |
| 50 g | *2 oz butter* |

Break the whites into a bowl, beat until stiff, beat in the castor sugar, add the flour, vanilla and softened butter. Grease a couple of thick non-stick baking sheets and distribute the mixture in small teaspoonfuls, with plenty of space between. Sprinkle shredded almonds on top of each. Bake to golden brown at 400°F 200°C gas 6, about 20 minutes, then lift off carefully with spatula and lay over a rolling pin to cool in a slightly curved shape.

  Can be prepared a day in advance and stored in an air-tight container.

# *Sunday Lunch*

## (for 6 people)

### CHICKEN LIVERS EN BROCHETTE

| 750 g | *1½ lb chicken livers* |
| 125 g | *4 oz lean rashers of bacon* |
| 225 g | *8 oz button mushrooms* |
|         | *1 large onion* |
|         | *3 bay leaves* |
|         | *Sunflower oil* |
|         | *Salt and pepper* |

6 flat skewers for serving

Allowing 4 oz (125 g) chicken livers per person, divide them into walnut-sized pieces and wrap each in a small strip of bacon. Brush (but do not peel) the mushrooms, slice the onion, snip the bay leaves into 3 sections each and thread everything on to 6 long flat skewers in the following order: mushroom, liver-in-bacon, onion, bay leaf, repeating until the skewers are firmly and equally filled, and finishing each with a final button mushroom.

  Brush over with oil and cook under the grill, turning the skewers from time to time until all is evenly cooked and the bacon crisp – about 10 minutes.

# Sunday Lunch

continued

BROWN RICE

225 g  *8 oz long-grain brown rice*
       *2 medium-sized onions*
       *Handful of sultanas*
25 g   *1 oz butter*
       *Salt*

Pour the brown rice into plenty of boiling salted water and simmer on low heat until tender but not soft (this will take nearly an hour). Put the sultanas in a small bowl and cover with boiling water, leaving them to soak for about 15 minutes, then drain.

Chop the onions and fry in the butter.

When the rice is done, drain it well in a sieve and mix together with the fried onions and sultanas. Reheat in a double boiler before serving.

## BONITA

       *4 eggs*
100 g  *4 oz castor sugar*
12 g   *½ oz leaf gelatine*
       *Rind and juice of 3 lemons*
       *Whipping cream*
       *Shredded and toasted almonds*

Soak the gelatine in water. When soft, drain and dissolve in lemon juice over low heat. Beat together the egg yolks, sugar and grated rind; gradually stir in the lemon juice. Whip the whites until stiff and fold in.

Stand the bowl in a larger bowl containing ice and water and stir until the mixture begins to thicken, then pour it into six glass goblets and refrigerate.*

When quite set cover with whipped cream and strew with lightly toasted shredded almonds. Serve with sponge fingers.

*This much can be prepared in advance.

# Sunday Supper

(for 2 people)

## SEA TROUT KEDGEREE

       *Remains of cold*
          *stuffed sea trout*
100 g  *4 oz Patna rice*
50 g   *2 oz butter*
       *1 onion, chopped*
       *1–2 hard-boiled eggs*
       *Seasoning, parsley*

Add the rice to plenty of boiling salted water, and cook for about 12 minutes. When done, drain thoroughly and return to the pan with the butter, chopped hard-boiled eggs, softened onion and flaked stuffed fish. Season well, stirring with a fork until all is well mixed and very hot.

Garnish with parsley and serve with a bowl of green salad.

# Antoinette Parkes

All my recipes are extremely quick and simple: perhaps this is because I do not enjoy cooking. If a new recipe looks as if it takes too long I do not attempt it. I find it hard to work in front of people: my concentration goes and I find I work too slowly, so I prepare everything I can in advance. If the odd meal has to be done at the last minute I choose a very quick recipe. I never seem to have a clear day, as I work part of the week, so I shop and cook on Thursdays and finish on Friday. I try to get most of the preparation done on Thursday, so by Friday I can just finish off and get the house organized.

Vegetables are best not prepared too long in advance (never cooked, just washed and chopped if necessary). If I am using a lot of salads I make up at least a pint of vinaigrette and chop huge bunches of parsley. Most dishes look much prettier simply garnished with parsley, watercress or mint.

I do find the Magimix an excellent aid, especially for pastry: I use ice-cold butter and make it very short. My deep freeze is a larder rather than a place to put pre-cooked food. I fill it with fish, meat, stocks, bread and ice creams. If I am pushed for time I abandon Saturday night pudding and get out a home-made ice cream. In July this might be rhubarb or gooseberry which I would have made in early summer and blackcurrant for January.

As far as wines are concerned I vary between French-bottled white Loire or Burgundy, which I drink before meals as well, and an English-bottled claret, almost never red Burgundy except perhaps for 'Nouveau'. At the moment the house white is Anton Rodet's Maître Rodet and the reds are 1962 Château Léoville Lascases, 1964 Château Grand-Puy-Lacoste, 1967 Château de Pez and 1970 Château Le Bon Pasteur.

I make my own bread for a weekend on the grounds that since I have to be in the kitchen I might as well, though I rarely bother mid-week as I have an excellent baker. Good bread is very important, not only for breakfast, but for cheese or soaking up stews, quite apart from the smell of home baking and the delicious sight of loaves cooling in the kitchen.

Breakfast is a meal I particularly dislike preparing, and I'm afraid none of my friends has the luxury of a cooked breakfast make to order. However, when they surface, they will always find my home-made bread, home-made marmalade, plum jam and a honey comb – and endless very strong freshly ground coffee, or tea, if they have warned me in advance. On

Saturday there is either a poached egg or a bowl of scrambled eggs, because both these keep warm without spoiling (provided you add a tablespoon or so of cream to the scrambled eggs when they have just cooked) and occasionally a fresh kipper. Always a boiled egg on Sunday and any fruit that I may have from the garden – plums, peaches, grapes, and in the autumn apples.

If at all possible, we eat breakfast outside in a splendid Edwardian loggia which in fact is my dining room throughout the summer. Being partly enclosed it is protected from the wind and rain. It faces south with a staggering view down the river Test, in the day lit by sunshine and in the evening by candles or moonlight.

## Friday

**SUPPER**

Egg and Onion Crumble

Pheasant and Chestnut Casserole
Mashed Potatoes
Cabbage cooked in Cream with Nutmeg

Hot Bread and Brie

## Saturday

**LUNCH**

Celery Soup and Croûtons

Bacon, Cider and Sausage Stew
Baked Potatoes
Carrots cooked in Butter

Cheese
Fruit and Nuts

**DINNER**

Green Almond Soup with Fried Almonds

Roast Teal (or Snipe or Woodcock)
Watercress and Green Salad
Fresh Orange and Onion Salad
Game Chips

Toffee Pudding

## Sunday

**LUNCH**

Braised Leg of Lamb (or Mutton)
Caper Sauce
Roast Potatoes
Brussels Sprouts

Lemon Meringue Pie

**SUPPER**

Gruyère Cheese Soufflé
Green Salad

Fresh Fruit

# Friday Supper

## (for 6 people)

### EGG AND ONION CRUMBLE

| | |
|---|---|
| | *10 eggs* |
| | *2 Spanish onions* |
| | *4 tablespoons fresh* |
| | *breadcrumbs* |
| 275 ml | *½ pint double cream* |
| | *Butter* |
| | *Seasoning* |

Boil the eggs for 10 minutes. Run them under cold water and peel. Separate the whites from the yolks and chop each finely. Make the breadcrumbs. Chop the onions roughly and soften in butter. Butter a 7-inch (18-cm) soufflé dish. Put in a layer of onions, egg whites, egg yolks, breadcrumbs and seasoning. Continue till dish is full, ending with a layer of breadcrumbs.*

To finish off the crumble, pour in the cream and place in hot oven for 20 minutes (400°F 200°C gas 6).

PREPARATION TIME: 25 minutes.

*This can be prepared a day in advance.

### PHEASANT AND CHESTNUT CASSEROLE

| | |
|---|---|
| | *1 large pheasant (or* |
| | *2 small ones)* |
| 25 g | *1 oz butter* |
| | *1 tablespoon olive oil* |
| 225 g | *1 tin of whole chestnuts* |
| 750 g | *1½ lb button onions* |
| 50 g | *2 scant oz flour* |
| 575 ml | *1 pint good beef stock* |
| | *Juice and grated rind* |
| | *of ½ orange* |
| | *1 dessertspoon of red* |
| | *currant jelly* |
| | *1 small glass red wine* |
| | *(or 1 teaspoon red wine* |
| | *vinegar)* |
| | *1 bay leaf* |
| | *Chopped parsley, seasoning* |

Brown the pheasant slowly in a casserole in oil and butter for about 15 minutes. Remove from the pan. Sauté the onions for a few minutes, then add chestnuts. Cook until they begin to colour, shaking pan frequently. Remove from the pan and add enough flour (off the heat) to take up the remaining fat. Mix well. Add the rest of the ingredients, except parsley, and bring to the boil. Put in the pheasant, surround with chestnuts and onions. Cover tightly. Cook in slow oven – 350°F 180°C gas 4 – for 1½–2 hours.

Take out and joint the bird and place in fresh casserole or deep dish with chestnuts and onions. Remove bay leaf, skim any fat from liquor, reduce if necessary. Adjust seasoning. Pour over pheasant.* Dust with parsley to serve.

PREPARATION TIME 30 minutes    COOKING TIME 2 hours.

*This can be made one or two days in advance. Reheat in moderate oven for about 35 minutes.

CABBAGE AND CREAM Shred a small white cabbage. Cook in frying pan with 2 tablespoons butter for 6 minutes. Pour in ¼ pint (150 ml) double cream, add freshly grated nutmeg and season.

MASHED POTATOES I add 2 tablespoons of cream, dot with butter and sprinkle with parsley.

Follow with Brie and hot bread.

# Saturday Lunch

## (for 6 people)

### CELERY SOUP

| | |
|---|---|
| 40 g | *1½ oz butter* |
| | *½ medium onion, chopped* |
| 225 g | *3 teacups of celery, thinly sliced* |
| | *(approx. ½ lb)* |
| | *1 medium potato, diced* |
| | *1 bay leaf* |
| 575 ml | *1 pint milk* |
| | *1 teaspoon salt* |
| | *Pepper* |
| | *Chopped parsley* |

Melt the butter, add the chopped onion and soften slowly without colouring. Add sliced celery and diced potato, salt, pepper and bay leaf. Cover with about a pint (575 ml) of water and simmer until vegetables are soft, about 30 minutes. Remove the bay leaf, add the milk and mix in liquidizer. Adjust seasoning.* Serve in individual bowls with a dessertspoonful of cream in each and garnished with parsley.

PREPARATION TIME 15 minutes.

* This much can be made a day or two in advance and reheated.

**CROUTONS**

*6 slices of white bread cut about ½″ (1 cm) thick*
*2 tablespoons of butter*

Remove crusts from bread and cut into ½″ (1 cm) cubes. Fry in butter until golden, about 3 minutes. Lift out of butter and keep warm.*

PREPARATION TIME 5 minutes.

*Can be made a day or two in advance and reheated in moderate oven for 10 minutes.

### BACON, CIDER AND SAUSAGE STEW

| | |
|---|---|
| 750 g | *1½ lb streaky bacon cut into 1″ (2 cm) cubes* |
| 750 g | *1½ lb pork sausages* |
| 150 ml | *¼ pint cider* |
| 150 g | *6 oz button onions (about 20)* |
| 575 ml | *1 pint chicken stock (a cube will do)* |
| | *Thyme or rosemary* |
| | *4 tablespoons oil* |
| | *2 tablespoons flour* |

Heat the oil in a casserole dish and brown the sausages, bacon and onions. Remove them from the pan, add the flour away from heat and mix well. Put back on heat and cook for a few minutes. Pour in the cider and stock, stirring all the time. Replace sausages, onions, bacon and thyme. Cook slowly over a low heat for 1½ hours. Put sausages, onions and bacon in clean casserole and strain the sauce over them.

This dish can be kept warm until ready or prepared a day or two in advance and reheated in a moderate oven for about ½ hour.

PREPARATION TIME 45 minutes.

**CARROTS COOKED IN BUTTER**

| | |
|---|---|
| 500 g | *1 lb carrots* |
| | *2 tablespoons butter* |
| | *Salt and pepper* |

Thinly slice the carrots. Melt butter in frying pan and cook carrots for about 4 minutes. Adjust seasoning. Keep warm till needed.

**BAKED POTATOES**

*6 large potatoes*
*Salt*

Wash the potatoes, rub them with salt, prick with a fork and bake in a hot oven, 450°F 230°C gas 8, for 1 hour.

# Saturday Dinner

(for 8 people)

## GREEN ALMOND SOUP

| | |
|---|---|
| 150 g | 6 oz ground almonds |
| 50 g | 2 oz flaked almonds (for the garnish) |
| | 2 tablespoons olive oil |
| | 1 small onion, finely chopped |
| 1 litre | 2 pints chicken stock (a cube will do) |
| | 2 level tablespoons cornflour |
| 275 ml | ½ pint milk |
| 150 ml | ¼ pint cream |
| | 2–3 teaspoons green colouring |
| | 1 bay leaf |
| | Salt |

This is a very old recipe and has a subtle flavour. The soup can be served white but I think it looks more appetizing with colouring added.

Soften the onion in oil. Do not brown. Stir in the ground almonds, stock, bay leaf and salt. Cook for ½ hour. Add the cold milk to the cornflour gradually in order to mix smoothly. Stir into soup and cook for a further 5 minutes, stirring frequently. Add cream and adjust seasoning. (It needs quite a bit of salt.) Remove bay leaf and mix in liquidizer. Pour into a bowl and add green colouring until it is pale avocado.*

Serve garnished with fried chopped almonds, made by frying split blanched almonds in 3 tablespoons of olive oil till golden.

PREPARATION TIME 15 minutes    COOKING TIME 30 minutes.

*Can be prepared in advance and reheated.

## ROAST TEAL (OR WOODCOCK, SNIPE, OR ANY SMALL GAME BIRD)

I always roast meat on a bed of vegetables. I find the meat does not dry up this way and it still gets crispy on top. You can also make a delicious stock or base of a sauce out of the vegetables and juice of the meat afterwards.

8 teal
2 carrots
1 onion
2 potatoes
4 oranges

Roughly chop onion, carrot and potato and put on the bottom of a roasting pan. Add about an inch (2 cm) of water. Cut the oranges in half and put one in each bird, and place the birds in the roasting pan. Roast in hot oven, 450°F 230°C gas 8, for 12 minutes if to be eaten rare and 15 minutes if you like them well done. Keep in warmer till required.

PREPARATION TIME 5 minutes    COOKING TIME 12–15 minutes.

WATERCRESS AND
GREEN SALAD

3 bunches watercress
1 lettuce
2 bunches spring onions
1 handful dill seeds

Remove most of the stalks from the watercress. Take the heart out of the lettuce and roughly shred. Clean spring onions and chop off roughly one-third of the green end. (They look prettier like this and are easy to pick up.) Mix well. Sprinkle over dill seeds and when ready to eat add vinaigrette made from 4 parts olive oil to 1 part tarragon vinegar, 1 teaspoon of French mustard, salt and freshly ground black pepper, and 1 tablespoon of parsley.

ORANGE, ONION AND
BLACK OLIVE SALAD

*4 juicy oranges*
*2 small onions or shallots*
*14 black olives*
*A dash of vinegar*

Peel and thinly slice the oranges. Slice the onion into rings. Put the oranges in a serving dish and mix in the onions. Scatter the olives on top and add a dash of vinegar.

GAME CHIPS

*8 medium-sized potatoes*
*Salt*

You will need to start cooking these at least an hour before you eat. I usually half-cook them well in advance.

Peel the potatoes and slice very finely. (Use a Magimix if you have one.) Heat the oil in a chip pan and cook the potatoes until transparent. You will probably have to do this in several batches. Put them on kitchen paper and leave to drain. Return chips to the hot oil (again in batches) and cook until golden brown and crispy. Drain again on kitchen paper, sprinkle with salt and keep warm. This last stage always takes longer than you think: allow at least 20 minutes. Once cooked, however, the chips will stay crispy for at least an hour.

PREPARATION TIME 10 minutes    COOKING TIME 30 minutes.

### TOFFEE PUDDING

This is one of the most delicious puddings, particularly popular with men. And it is very easy to make. It can be made an hour before eating and kept warm, or made the day before and reheated. If you do this reserve a little of the sauce separately and pour it over the pudding after it has been warmed through to moisten the bread.

|   |   |
|---|---|
|        | *1 loaf of thick sliced* |
|        | *white bread* |
| 450 g  | *1 lb butter* |
| 450 g  | *1 lb demerara sugar* |
| 750 g  | *1½ lb golden syrup* |
| 575 ml | *1 pint double cream, whipped* |
| 275 ml | *½ pint milk* |

Cut the crust off the bread and chop it into thick fingers about 2 inches (5 cm) long by 1 inch (2 cm) wide. Place in a large flat dish. Heat the butter, demerara sugar and syrup gently in a large frying pan. Stir until melted, then boil more rapidly until golden brown, stirring continuously.

Bring the milk to boiling point and pour it over the fingers of bread. Lift them out at once and put them into the toffee sauce. Coat them well. Pile them into a flat fireproof dish (I use a large white china flan dish) and pour on any left-over sauce. Cover and keep warm.* Serve with a bowl of whipped cream.

*Can be made in advance and reheated, covered, in a moderate oven for ½ hour.

# Sunday Lunch

## (for 6 people)

### BRAISED LEG OF LAMB OR MUTTON

*1 large leg of lamb*
*2 carrots*
*1 large onion*
*2 potatoes*

If you have a lot of people to feed, and you can get a leg of mutton instead of lamb, so much the better.

Chop vegetables roughly and place meat on them in a roasting tin. Surround with about 1 inch (2 cm) water. Roast in a hot oven, 450°F 230°C gas 8, for 20 minutes per lb (450 g).
    Serve accompanied by caper sauce.

### CAPER SAUCE

20 g   *¾ oz butter*
20 g   *¾ oz flour*
275 ml   *½ pint vegetable stock*
         *or water*
       *1 teaspoon wine vinegar*
       *½ teaspoon made mustard*
       *Salt and pepper*
       *1 large tablespoon capers*
22 g   *1½ tablespoons cream*

Melt the butter in a saucepan, remove from heat and add the flour. Pour in the stock and vinegar, mustard, seasonings and capers. Stir until boiling and cook for 5 minutes. Adjust seasoning. Add cream and serve.
    This be made a day or so in advance and reheated. Cover the sauce with cling film to prevent a skin forming.
    Caper sauce is also delicious with boiled chicken: pour it over the chicken when serving.

### ROAST POTATOES

*4 small potatoes per person*
*Cooking oil*

Peel the potatoes and chop in half if necessary so that all the pieces are the same sort of size. Bring to the boil and cook for 8 minutes. Take out, dry and scour all over with a fork. Put in a roasting dish and surround with fresh oil. Roast for 1 hour, turning once. It is always best to eat them at once while they are crisp, but if you do have to keep them, turn oven down and keep them in the oil until you serve them.

**PREPARATION TIME** 10 minutes   **COOKING TIME** 1 hour.

### BRUSSELS SPROUTS

1 kg   *2 lb fresh or 2 large packets*
       *frozen Brussels sprouts*
     *1 tablespoon grated Parmesan*
       *cheese*

Trim and wash the sprouts and cook in boiling salted water for 7 minutes. Drain and put in dish, dot with butter and sprinkle with Parmesan. Cover and keep warm.

### LEMON MERINGUE PIE

This can be eaten hot or cold. I always use a Magimix to make the pastry: it takes 5 minutes and tastes delicious.

SHORTCRUST PASTRY

350 g  *12 oz flour*
110 g  *4½ oz margarine*
40 g  *1½ oz lard*
     *6 tablespoons ice-cold water*
     *1 teaspoon sugar*

To make by hand, sift flour into bowl, chop fat and mix with finger tips until it looks like breadcrumbs. Add sugar and then water. Mix with a palette knife until the moment when the mixture begins to form into small lumps of dough. Then knead it together by hand into a ball. Cover with greaseproof paper and put in fridge for ½ hour.

Line an 8-inch (20-cm) white china flan dish with pastry and roll your rolling pin over the edges to get a smooth top. Prick the bottom with a fork.* Line with tin foil and fill with a handful or so of rice. Bake blind in a hot oven, 400°F 200°C gas 6, for 10 minutes. Take out, cool and fill.

*This much can be prepared in advance.

LEMON FILLING
AND MERINGUE

     *2 tablespoons cornflour*
     *½ teaspoon salt*
195 g  *7 oz sugar*
275 ml  *½ pint boiling water*
     *1 scant tablespoon butter*
     *4½ tablespoons lemon juice*
     *Grated rind of ½ lemon*
     *3 egg yolks, lightly beaten*
     *3 egg whites*
     *1 tablespoon castor sugar*

Combine the cornflour, salt, sugar and water in a double saucepan and heat, stirring continuously, until mixture boils. Reduce heat and simmer for 15 minutes, occasionally stirring. Beat in lemon juice and rind. Stir in egg yolks, and continue cooking until mixture thickens. Cool.*

If you plan to eat the pie hot, pour the filling into the baked pastry shell half an hour before serving. Whip up egg whites until very stiff, so that the peaks stand up, fold in the sugar and pile meringue on to the pie. Bake in a hot oven, 450°F 230°C gas 8, for 20 minutes or until golden.

PREPARATION TIME 30 minutes.

*If you wish, the filling can now be set aside for a day.

# Sunday Supper

(for 2 people)

### GRUYERE CHEESE SOUFFLE

Soufflés should be eaten the instant they are cooked. They are not difficult to make, but do not open the oven half way through to see how your soufflé is getting on: a draught will make it flop. The addition of Gruyère or Stilton makes all the difference to the flavour of this cheese soufflé.

2 tablespoons butter
1 tablespoon flour
2½ tablespoons Cheddar
1 tablespoon Gruyère
275 ml ½ pint milk
2 egg yolks
4 egg whites
Salt and pepper
15 ml 1 tablespoon of cream (optional)

Melt the butter, and add the flour off the heat. Mix well and gradually blend in the milk. Stir in the cheeses and seasonings.* Cool slightly.

Stir in the egg yolks until well mixed. Whip the whites very very stiff. Pour on top of mixture and fold in, using a metal spoon. Pour mixture into a 5-inch (15-cm) greased soufflé dish and cook in hot oven, 450°F 230°C gas 8, for exactly ½ hour.

PREPARATION TIME 15 minutes.

Serve with a green salad.

*This much can be prepared a day in advance and set aside, covered with greaseproof paper or cling film.

*Georgia Langton's house in the West Country
is the remains of a medieval Augustinian priory
which was converted into a farmhouse at the
Dissolution of the monasteries in the 1530s.
A considerable portion of the original
thirteenth- to fifteenth-century buildings survives.*

# FEBRUARY

—◄◆►—

# Georgia Langton

Georgia never shops for a weekend. Her kitchen is filled with provisions. Huge jars of lentils and beans, pasta, lots of different mustards (nettle and green peppercorn) and oils. She says: 'I always use vegetable oils and mix them with virgin pressed green olive oil and walnut oil for flavour.

'My deep freeze is full of meat and bread and at least four stocks – veal, fish, game and chicken. I would either have a day stock-making, or when cooking game, for instance, would use my deep freeze one for the sauce and replace it with a new one made from the duck carcase later on. I purée certain vegetables for soup – the celeriac soup for Sunday supper I would have as a vegetable during the week, purée the rest and freeze until needed.

We eat only local cheese, which I buy in the cloth: it keeps for ages. My dairy produce is delivered and I bulk-buy provisions every six months or so. I look forward to the first pickings of fruits or baby beans. It is much more exciting than having them all the year. I freeze some herbs. Tarragon, basil just picked and boxed without blanching, and blocks of parsley, chopped and then frozen (you can scrape it off as you need it).' She also keeps lots of dried herbs, and *cèpe* mushrooms which have a much stronger flavour for sauce making then fresh ones.

'I make lots of pickles with blackberries and ghurkins. Jams too, and I bottle fruit like peaches or pears in brandy.'

As far as Georgia is concerned breakfast is a non-event. The table is laid and guests who wish to have a cooked breakfast can make their own, but there are always fresh farm eggs, brown bread, honey and jams – and a large pot of coffee on the Aga which is kept filled all morning.

Georgia eats and cooks in a huge forty-foot room and loves having people around her when cooking. 'Then I never feel excluded.' She tends not to cook a very complicated dish for weekends since 'some sauces often need attention at the last minute'. The food is good home cooking.

'I would probably do the menus on Wednesday. I try not to have a routine of any description, so when someone extra arrives I am not thrown. My food is always elastic. I never start cooking for the weekend before Friday but then sometimes half-cook things in advance – not a cassoulet or stew (these are better reheated) – but the duck breasts I would cook for ten minutes and then joint the bird, so that it is never overcooked when warming up. I do not like puddings, so rarely use them, and often exclude potatoes because I love the look of only two portions of food on a plate.

'I always serve everything myself and can then garnish the plate at the same time. The duck on Saturday looks delicious with bite-sized crunchy vegetables, garnished with watercress.

Georgia's favourite wines are Sancerre – a dry white wine from the Loire valley – Brouilly, which is a good Beaujolais, or a claret like 1971 Pomerol.

She says: 'I love cooking and my life revolves around it. One of my greatest pleasures is reading a good cook book.'

### Friday

**SUPPER**

Hot Cheese Croûtons

Lamb Chump Chops with Garlic and Brandy
Jerusalem Artichokes

Green Salad with Walnuts
Strong Cheddar

### Saturday

**LUNCH**

Boiling Sausage
Hot Potato Salad

Baked Apples in Puff Pastry
Home Made Custard

**DINNER**

Flamiche aux Poireaux

Duck Breasts with Fresh Green Peppercorns
Roast Potatoes
Roast Turnips and Apples

Hot Black Cherries in Brandy
Coffee or Herb Tea

### Sunday

**LUNCH**

Cassoulet with Haricot Beans
Green Salad

Fresh Fruit

**SUPPER**

Celeriac and Dill Soup

Grilled Duck Legs
Green Salad

# Friday Supper

## (for 6 people)

### HOT CHEESE CROUTONS

6 slices granary bread
6 slices strong Cheddar
French mustard
2 tins anchovy fillets
  and/or raw onion slices
Black olives

Butter the slices of bread and spread fairly thickly with French mustard. Top with a slice of cheese and finish with either an anchovy fillet or a small slice of raw onion. Slice into 'soldiers' or quarters, arrange on large baking tray.

Put into hot oven, 425–450°F 220–230°C gas 7–8, for approximately 5 minutes, or until cheese has melted, and serve with drinks before supper with a bowl of black olives.

PREPARATION All done in morning

### LAMB CHUMP CHOPS WITH GARLIC AND BRANDY

6 very thick lamb chops
14 cloves garlic, peeled
225 ml 8 fluid oz brandy
Stock cube dissolved in
  8 fluid oz (225 ml) water
Black pepper and salt

Do not be put off by the amount of garlic in this recipe. After the lengthy cooking it will have almost disintegrated. I usually mash it up with the juice just before serving in case the sight of so many cloves has our guests diving for their cars.

Brown the chops in a large casserole in butter over a fairly high heat. Add warmed brandy, flame it and when flames have died down add the garlic, stock and black pepper and boil for a few minutes until the liquid has reduced by a third. Cover with lid and cook in a low oven, 275–300°F 140–150°C gas 1–2, until tender – about $1\frac{1}{2}$–$2\frac{1}{2}$ hours depending on thickness of chops. Season to taste with salt.

Can be prepared in the morning or day before.

### JERUSALEM ARTICHOKES

5 or 6 Jerusalem artichokes
  per person
Parsley, chopped
Salt and pepper

This method ought to insure against overcooking the artichokes.

Peel the artichokes. Bring to the boil in salted water and cook for approximately 3 minutes. Strain and finish cooking in a covered pan in butter with salt and pepper over a low heat, making sure they don't stick. Be careful not to overcook them: they should still be quite firm. But don't despair if they do go all mushy and fall to pieces. Liquidize them, add some left-over mashed potatoes and serve as a purée – just as good. Garnish with parsley.

### VINAIGRETTE SAUCE

1 rounded teaspoon French
  mustard
Salt and pepper
1 dessertspoon wine vinegar
4 tablespoons olive oil
1 dessertspoon walnut oil

### GREEN SALAD WITH WALNUTS AND STRONG CHEDDAR

Plain green salad or mixed green salad. Handful of walnuts
Toss salad with dressing and sprinkle walnuts on top.

Serve and eat together with strong Cheddar.

# Saturday Lunch

(for 6 people)

---

## BOILING SAUSAGE

*About 3 large Frankfurter-
type boiling sausages –
depending on size*

If in packet follow instructions, otherwise prick the sausages all over to stop them splitting and simmer for 20–30 minutes in water.

### HOT POTATO SALAD

*2 or 3 potatoes per person
1 coffee cup wine vinegar
Olive oil
Black pepper and salt
1 large finely sliced onion*

Steam or simmer the unpeeled potatoes until only just cooked. They must remain firm. Leave until cool enough to handle, then peel and slice, not too thinly. While still warm pour over wine vinegar. Season with salt and a lot of black pepper and finally sprinkle on some olive oil and add the sliced onion.

Serve while still warm on a large dish with the sausages piled up in the middle. Make sure you have a large pot of good French mustard on the table, and big tankards of cool beer.

## BAKED APPLES IN PUFF PASTRY

*6 large dessert apples*
350 g *12 oz packet frozen puff pastry*
*Honey
Chopped almonds
Powdered cinnamon
Lemon
Sultanas
Egg white to seal
Egg yolk to glaze*

Peel and core the apples and powder them with cinnamon. Divide pastry into six and roll out very thinly, making each piece as square as possible. Place each apple in centre of square of pastry and fill the centre with a mixture of sultanas and chopped almonds and a spoonful of honey. Squeeze on some lemon juice. Wrap the pastry round, bringing the four corners together and sealing them with egg white. Decorate with a pastry leaf if you have some pastry to spare. Glaze with egg yolk.

Cook in a moderate oven 350–400°F 180–190°C gas 4–5 for 10 minutes; then when pastry has risen turn oven down to 325–350°F 170–180°C gas 3–4 for another 15–20 minutes, depending on size of apples.

Serve with freshly made custard flavoured with vanilla, or thick double cream.

### CUSTARD

*2 egg yolks*
275 ml *½ pint milk
½ tablespoon of sugar
½ vanilla pod*

Beat the egg yolks with a fork. Put the sugar, milk and vanilla pod in a saucepan and bring to the boil. Remove the vanilla pod and pour the milk slowly on to the egg yolks, stirring all the time. Return to the pan. Stir over a moderate heat until the mixture coats the back of the spoon.

---

# Saturday Dinner

## (for 8 people)

---

### FLAMICHE AUX POIREAUX

This quantity will serve 8 people as a starter or 4 as a main course.

| | |
|---|---|
| 500 g | *1 lb white part of leeks* |
| 40 g | *1½ oz unsalted butter* |
| 275 ml | *10 fluid oz carton double cream* |
| 400 g | *14 oz packet frozen flaky pastry* |
| | *Lemon juice and rind* |
| | *Salt, freshly ground pepper and grated nutmeg* |
| | *1 egg, beaten* |

Divide pastry into two equal parts. Have it soft enough to roll very thinly. Cut 2 circles with a 9-inch (22-cm) flan ring. Set in fridge to cool.*

Clean and chop leeks into equal, small parts. Melt unsalted butter in a large sauté pan over heat. Cook leeks till soft, stirring all the time – they must not brown. When soft add cream; increase heat. Boil hard till cream is reduced to half original amount. Add lemon rind, juice, salt, pepper and grated nutmeg. Allow the filling to cool: it gets thicker and easier to manage as it cools.*

Put the leeks in the centre of one pastry round. Dampen the edges. Place remaining round on top. Seal the edges. Frill with a knife to make rising easier, and brush with beaten egg.

Put into hot oven, 450°F 230°C gas 8, for 10 minutes, then reduce heat to 375°F 190°C gas 5 for a further 20 minutes.

Serve piping hot. Cut like a cake.

*Up to this stage it can be prepared several hours in advance.

### DUCK BREASTS WITH FRESH GREEN PEPPERCORNS

| | |
|---|---|
| | *4 Aylesbury ducks (3 if very fat)* |
| | *16 tablespoons dry white wine* |
| | *5 tablespoons armagnac or brandy (extra for duck breasts)* |
| | *8 tablespoons stock* |
| 475 ml | *¾ pint double cream* |
| 50 g | *2 oz green peppercorns* |
| | *Salt and pepper* |
| | *Bunch of watercress* |

Sprinkle duck with salt and pepper and put into a very hot oven, 450°F 230°C gas 8, for 10 minutes. Remove, and when cool enough to handle remove breasts from breast bone with a very sharp flexible knife. Take off the skin and carve the breasts into very thin slices across the grain. The flesh will still be extremely pink – don't panic; sprinkle each slice with a few drops of brandy, season with black pepper, wrap in tin foil and put in fridge until needed.

Joint the rest of the duck, put legs and wings in foil in fridge to be used on Sunday night and make stock with the carcase. Keep fat separate and use for roasting the vegetables.

To make the sauce: bring white wine and brandy to the boil and reduce by two-thirds (approximately 5 minutes). Add the stock (use a chicken stock cube if you have not had time to make it from the carcase) and boil for another 5 minutes. Add the double cream, season lightly with salt and pepper and reduce again by a third. The sauce should have thickened.*

Remove breasts from fridge – lay in a shallow serving dish. Reheat

---

# Saturday Dinner

## continued

sauce carefully and add the fresh green peppercorns. Pour over the breasts and put in a cool oven, 200°–250°F 110–130°C gas $\frac{1}{4}$–$\frac{1}{2}$, long enough to warm the breasts through. The heat of the sauce will finish cooking the breasts, although they should be just slightly pink and tender. Do not add the peppercorns before the final heating or you will make the sauce far too peppery.

*Can be prepared up to this point in the morning.

### ROAST POTATOES, ROAST TURNIPS AND ROAST APPLES

*1 potato*
*1 dessert apple*  } per
*1 turnip*          person
*Lemon juice*

Peel potatoes and turnips and blanch in boiling water for 5 minutes. Cut into large cubes and put in roasting pan with duck fat. Peel and dice the apples and put in water with lemon juice added to keep white. Roast the diced potatoes and turnips in a hot oven 425–450°F 220–230°C gas 7–8 until brown and add the apples just 10 minutes before serving so that they remain firm.

TO SERVE Lay two or three thin slices of duck breast on each plate. Cover with a little of the sauce and peppercorns. Arrange a mixture of vegetables around the meat and garnish with fresh watercress.

### HOT BLACK CHERRIES IN BRANDY

2 × 200 g  *2 × 15 oz tins black cherries*
*Large wineglass brandy*
*1 dessertspoon rice flour*
*Thick double cream or*
*   vanilla ice cream*

Strain the cherries. Add brandy to the cherry juice and heat. Mix rice flour with cold water and add to warmed juice. Heat till thickened.*
   Divide black cherries into 8 ovenproof ramekins. Pour hot sauce over them and keep hot in oven. Serve with a large blob of thick double cream or vanilla ice cream on top of each ramekin.

*Can be prepared in morning or day before and reheated.

Follow by freshly made strong black coffee or lime or mint tea.

# Sunday Lunch

## CASSOULET

| | |
|---|---|
| 1 kg | *2 lb white haricot beans* |
| 500 g | *1 lb garlic sausage* |
| 1¼ kg | *2½ lb pork spare rib* |
| | *or bladebone* |
| 750 g | *1½ lb shoulder lamb* |
| 250 g | *8 oz green bacon in the* |
| | *piece* |
| | *Onion* |
| | *Bay leaf, thyme, parsley* |
| | *Garlic* |
| | *Salt and pepper* |
| | *Breadcrumbs* |

I make enormous quantities of this as it reheats very well and can be made on Friday. This recipe feeds 18 people!

Soak the beans overnight. Remove the rind from bacon and pork and cut into small squares. Add these to the beans with the onion, bacon, all the herbs and the garlic. Cover with water and boil for approximately 1 hour, adding the garlic sausage half way through.

Roast the pork and lamb gently until not quite cooked – about 10 minutes to the lb (450 g). Cut into pieces.

Drain the bean mixture and keep the liquid. Put a layer of the bean mixture in the bottom of a casserole and add both kinds of meat. Put the rest of the beans etc. on top and moisten with half of the reserved liquid. Cover with a thick layer of breadcrumbs and cook without a lid in a slow oven, 250°F 130°C gas ½, for 1½ hours at least. The breadcrumbs should make a lovely crust on top and the beans stay creamy underneath. If during this last bit of cooking the beans start looking dry, add some more of the reserved liquid. (There is nothing worse than trying to eat a plateful of dry cassoulet.)

Serve on really hot plates with iced *Beaujolais Nouveau* and a green salad. With a bit of luck no one will need a pudding after it. Just masses of fresh black coffee and a long siesta.

# Sunday Supper

(for 2 people)

## CELERIAC AND DILL SOUP

| | |
|---|---|
| 250–500 g | *1 celeriac, about 8–12 oz* |
| 850 ml | *1½ pints chicken stock* |
| | *2 cooked potatoes* |
| | *Dried dill weed to taste* |
| | *(or fennel)* |
| | *Black pepper* |
| | *Single cream* |

This soup serves 6, and can be frozen without the cream.

Boil celeriac in the stock with the dill weed till tender. Liquidize with the potato and the stock* and serve with thin cream and lots of black pepper stirred in at the last moment.

*Can be prepared in advance.

## GRILLED DUCK LEGS

Cover the duck legs with a layer of French mustard and lots of salt and roll them in breadcrumbs. Put under the grill or in a very hot oven until cooked – about 20 minutes – and eat in your fingers with a plateful of mixed green salad with a lot of watercress in it.

# Sally Worthington

Sally lives in an isolated farmhouse with low, timbered rooms. It is always filled with flowers and everything in it is immaculate. Her kitchen is small and she cooks on an electric cooker.

'Our friends who come for weekends are usually people who appreciate good cooking. I enjoy cooking enormously. I usually shop on Thursday, cook all the rest of that day and finish on Friday. There is never enough time to cook it all on one day without being exhausted.

'My deep freeze is used for keeping demi-glace for sauces, and purées, a good quantity of stock and some pre-cooked foods, but this is usually for children. I also use it for teas – sticky chocolate cake, flapjacks or walnut layered cake. People usually say they don't want tea until it is offered and then eat it all.' Some of Sally's favourite teatime cake recipes are included here.

'I shop locally, but always have a stock of pistachio nuts, green peppercorns, etc. which I find difficult to get locally. I also ask my friends to bring me down a delicious cheese if they are coming from London. On Friday nights I never have a pudding, and rarely a stew as my husband doesn't like them. It is also the one night when I can cook up to the time we eat, as people are invariably late, so I choose something that can be done easily and quickly at the last minute.

'If I am having to do cold food, which on the whole men do not like, I would always make it substantial, i.e. cold pies, joints etc. I often have a separate menu for children, usually because they want to eat at a different time from us; we often lunch after 2 o'clock, by which time they are starving. It also gets them out of the way on Saturday nights when I am trying to cook for a dinner party.'

Sally has breakfast in the kitchen and cooks for people as and when they appear. There is always a pot of good coffee kept warm all morning, delicious bread and home-made jam. She finds however that few women like a cooked breakfast and most of her friends like to stay in bed until mid-morning, with the exception of bachelors who almost always want to get up and eat a huge cooked meal, which might then be home-made sausages, fried eggs, tomatoes and bacon.

|            | **SUPPER** |
| *Friday*   | Leeks in Leek Sauce |
|            | Game Pie |
|            | Celeriac and Mashed Potatoes |
|            | Herbed Carrots |
|            | Cheese |

*Friday*

**SUPPER**

Leeks in Leek Sauce

Game Pie
Celeriac and Mashed Potatoes
Herbed Carrots

Cheese

*Saturday*

**LUNCH**

Lasagne
Salad of Celery, Corn Salad, White Chicory and Red Chicory

Apricot and Almond Crumble

**DINNER**

Artichoke Mousse and Mayonnaise Sauce

Loin of Lamb with Chestnut Stuffing and Chasseur Sauce
Cauliflower and Watercress Purée
Roast Potatoes

Chocolate Cream Pie

*Sunday*

**LUNCH**

Roast Pork (cooked like Game)
Baked Apples
Roast Potatoes
Broccoli

Treacle Tart and Cream

**SUPPER**

Mushroom and Mustard Soup
Hot Bread

Cold Pork
Red Cabbage Salad

# Friday Supper

## (for 6 people)

### LEEKS IN LEEK SAUCE

2–3 *thin leeks per person and 3 extra for the sauce*
35 g   *1½ oz butter*
*Juice of 1 lemon*

SAUCE

*½ teaspoon castor sugar*
*1 dessertspoon Moutarde de Meaux*
*2 tablespoons chopped parsley*
*1 tablespoon chopped chives*
150 ml   *¼ pint olive oil*
*1 tablespoon wine vinegar*
*1 hard-boiled egg*
*Herbs for the garnish*

Put all the leeks in a buttered ovenproof dish, dab with a little more butter, pour over the lemon juice and cover with water. Season and bake in the oven at 400°F 200°C gas 6 for about 30 minutes. They should still be slightly firm. Cool in the liquid, then strain and put in serving dish, reserving 3 leeks for the sauce.

To make the sauce, put the 3 extra leeks in a Magimix or liquidizer with the castor sugar, mustard, parsley, chives, olive oil and the wine vinegar. Blend. If necessary thin with a little of the leek liquid. Pour over the leeks and chill.* Before serving sprinkle with a few more herbs and a chopped hard-boiled egg.

PREPARATION AND COOKING TIME 40 minutes.

*This much can be done the day before.

### GAME PIE

RICH RAISED PIE CRUST

450 g   *1 lb plain flour*
*1 teaspoon salt*
*4 tablespoons butter*
*4 tablespoons lard*
*2 egg yolks*
*Salt and pepper*
*A little water*

FILLING

*1 boned pheasant*
*Nutmeg*
*Allspice*
*Cloves*
*2 tablespoons chopped parsley*
*1 teaspoon lemon thyme (or grated rind of ½ lemon with thyme)*
500 g   *1 lb sausagemeat*
500 g   *1 lb cooked ham in one piece*
*1 beaten egg*

Knead all the ingredients together or mix in a Magimix. Wrap in muslin or greaseproof paper and put in the fridge for ½ hour. Line a well buttered raised pie mould or a high-sided 8-inch (20-cm) pie dish with two-thirds of the pastry. Reserve the rest to make a lid.

Roughly chop the ham. Bone pheasant (page 47) or get the butcher to do it. Season the flesh side with salt and pepper, ground nutmeg, allspice and cloves. Add a good handful of parsley and lemon thyme, then spread with a layer of sausagemeat and half of the ham. Roll up the pheasant and fit into the mould (if the pheasant is very large cut it in half). Fill in any spaces with the rest of the ham and sausagemeat and any left-over herbs. Wet the edges of the pie and put on the lid, pinching well round the edges. Cut a largish hole in the middle and decorate with pastry leaves. Sprinkle with sea salt and brush with a beaten egg.

Bake the pie in a hot oven, 450°F 230°C gas 8, until the top is brown, then cover loosely with foil and reduce the heat to 375°F 190°C gas 5 for 2 hours. Take out and cool. Meanwhile make a good strong stock from the bones and trimmings, which should gel when cold. Pour this through the hole in the middle of the pie.

PREPARATION TIME 1 hour.

Should be made the day before and keeps very well.

CELERIAC AND
MASHED POTATOES

| | |
|---|---|
| 500 g | *1 lb celeriac* |
| 500 g | *1 lb potatoes* |
| 150 ml | *¼ pint double cream* |
| 25 g | *1 oz butter* |
| | *Salt and pepper* |
| | *Parsley for garnishing* |

Peel and cook the potatoes. Scrub the celeriac and cook till tender, about 35 minutes, then peel. Put the potatoes and celeriac through a Mouli or food processor. Add the cream, butter, salt and pepper.* Sprinkle with chopped parsley to serve.

*This can be made in advance and reheated.

HERBED CARROTS

| | |
|---|---|
| | *8 medium-sized carrots* |
| | *1 tablespoon sugar* |
| 50 g | *2 oz butter* |
| | *3 tablespoons chopped parsley, chives etc.* |
| | *Chicken stock* |
| | *Salt and pepper* |

Slice the carrots lengthwise and cook in the chicken stock until just tender, about 7 minutes. Drain and sprinkle with herbs, sugar and butter. Toss over the heat until the butter and sugar have melted. Add salt and pepper. These will keep warm, covered, in a very low oven.

Follow by Farmhouse Cheddar and homemade oatmeal biscuits (see page 20).

## HOW TO BONE AND STUFF ANY BIRD

This is well worth doing yourself, and is much easier than it sounds. Once you have mastered the technique you can bone any bird.

Place bird breast-side down on a wooden board. Take a small *very* sharp knife. If there is a claw or a bit of meatless bone on the end of the leg cut it off. Slit the bird open (through bones and flesh) from head to tail. Cut off wing joints and keep for another meal. From inside the bird, cut the drumstick bone at the joint with body, taking care not to cut through the skin; from here now work back flesh towards the end of the leg with the tip of knife. Cut tendons round next leg joint and work rest of flesh away from bone. You can now pull the bone out of the leg. Repeat this on the other leg.

With tip of knife work directly along bones of rib cage, down towards the breast, easing flesh from bones. As you reach the top of the breast, again taking care not to puncture the skin (if necessary leave a little of soft top breast bone in carcase). Work along to wishbone. You now have a flattish carcase and a detached skeleton.

# Saturday Lunch

## (for 6 people)

### LASAGNE

| | |
|---|---|
| 150 g | *5 oz green lasagne* |
| | *1 large onion* |
| 270 g | *10 oz tin tomatoes* |
| | *1 tablespoon tomato purée* |
| 75 g | *3 oz bacon* |
| 750 g | *1½ lb good minced beef* |
| 150 ml | *¼ pint white wine* |
| 150 ml | *¼ pint stock* |
| | *Marjoram* |
| | *Parsley* |
| | *Salt and pepper* |
| | *Béchamel sauce (see page 153* |
| | *but use 1 pint (575 ml)* |
| | *of milk and 2 oz (50 g)* |
| | *Cheddar)* |

It is important to use good minced beef for lasagne. Get your butcher to mince it for you. You can vary this recipe by making the cheese sauce with Gruyère and a little mustard, or add a beaten egg to the sauce or cottage cheese and a beaten egg, depending on what you have in the fridge.

Chop the bacon and onion. Fry the bacon until the fat runs and add the onion, a little butter and oil if necessary and then the mince. Fry until browned. Add the wine, stock, tin of tomatoes, tomato purée, salt, pepper, marjoram and parsley and simmer for 30 minutes.

Make 1 pint of Béchamel sauce. Butter a large shallow ovenproof dish. Cook the lasagne in plenty of boiling salted water with a little oil till tender, about 12 minutes. Drain and put a layer of the meat mixture in an ovenproof dish, cover with a layer of cheese sauce, then a layer of lasagne. Repeat, finishing with cheese sauce on top.* Sprinkle with a little Parmesan and cook in a moderate oven until brown on top.

PREPARATION TIME 45 minutes.

*This can be made the day before and reheated. It freezes very well.

### WINTER SALAD

*Red chicory*
*Corn salad*
*Celery*
*White chicory*

I get my red chicory and corn salad from the garden, and celery and white chicory from the greengrocer.

Chop all the ingredients, put in the fridge to crisp up if necessary and serve with a vinaigrette sauce.

### APRICOT AND ALMOND CRUMBLE

#### CRUMBLE

| | |
|---|---|
| 125 g | *4 oz plain flour* |
| 125 g | *4 oz castor sugar* |
| 125 g | *4 oz ground almonds* |
| 125 g | *4 oz butter* |

#### FILLING

| | |
|---|---|
| 750 g | *1½ lb fresh apricots,* |
| | *or 2 large tins* |
| | *1 handful of split almonds* |
| | *for garnishing* |

Mix the crumble together with your fingertips until it resembles breadcrumbs.*

Stone apricots, put them in a shallow ovenproof dish and sprinkle on the crumble mixture. Decorate with split almonds. Bake in a hot oven, 400°F 200°C gas 6, for 30 minutes.

PREPARATION TIME 12 minutes.

*This can be done in advance.

# Saturday Dinner

## (for 8 people)

### ARTICHOKE MOUSSE AND MAYONNAISE SAUCE

| | |
|---|---|
| 1 kg | *2 lb Jerusalem artichokes* |
| 50 g | *2 oz gelatine* |
| | *6 tablespoons water* |
| | *Juice of 1 lemon* |
| 275 ml | *½ pint double cream* |
| | *Nutmeg* |
| | *Salt and pepper* |
| | *3 egg whites* |
| | *1 avocado pear* |
| 125 g | *4 oz button mushrooms* |
| | *Vinaigrette made from lemon juice,* |
| | *olive oil and parsley* |
| | *Mayonnaise:* |
| | *see page 116* |
| | *but use ¾ pint (425 ml)* |
| | *of olive oil* |

Oil a 2–2½-pint (1-litre) tin mould with a hole in the centre. Cook the artichokes until tender, cool and peel them. Liquidize till smooth. Dissolve the gelatine in the water and lemon juice. Add to the purée. Whip the double cream until it is floppy, fold into the purée and season with nutmeg, salt and pepper. Beat the egg whites till stiff and fold them in gently. Put into the mould and leave till set, about 3 hours.*

Turn out just before serving – plunge into hot water for a few seconds if the mousse does not slide out – and fill the centre with raw sliced mushrooms and avocado tossed in lemon juice, oil and parsley.

Serve with mayonnaise thinned with white wine or Vermouth.

PREPARATION TIME 40 minutes.

*The mousse can be made a day in advance, and the filling prepared just before dinner.

### LOIN OF LAMB WITH CHESTNUT STUFFING AND CHASSEUR SAUCE

| | |
|---|---|
| 1¼ kg | *2½ lb boned loin of lamb* |
| | *1 medium onion* |
| | *Oil and butter* |
| 250 g | *8 oz minced belly of pork* |
| | *3 tablespoons unsweetened chestnut purée* |
| | *3 tablespoons chopped herbs – lemon thyme, parsley, marjoram etc* |
| | *Salt and pepper* |
| | *1 glass of white wine* |
| | |
| | SAUCE |
| 275 ml | *½ pint demi-glace sauce (see page 120)* |
| | *3 tomatoes, peeled, de-seeded and chopped* |
| | *A little stock* |

The lamb can be stuffed and the demi-glace sauce made the day before. I usually have this in large quantities in the deep freeze and just get out the amount I need.

Score the inside of the meat and season well. Chop the onion and fry until soft, add the minced pork, chestnut purée, herbs and seasoning and spread over the surface of the meat. Roll up the meat and tie well with string. Spread the outside of the meat with butter and pepper, put into a roasting dish and pour the white wine around it. Roast in a hot oven 450°F 230°C gas 8 for 1–1¼ hours, depending on how pink you like it. Remove from the oven and keep warm.

Pour off the fat from the pan and de-glaze (see page 116) with a little stock, add the demi-glace sauce and tomatoes and boil for 2 minutes. Slice the meat, spoon a little of the sauce over it and hand the rest separately.

# Saturday Dinner

## continued

---

CAULIFLOWER AND
WATERCRESS PUREE
*1 large or 2 small
  cauliflowers*
*2 bunches watercress*
150 ml    *¼ pint double cream*
275 ml    *½ pint milk*
*1 tablespoon flour*
*1 tablespoon butter*
*Salt and pepper*

Separate the cauliflower into branches. Cook in boiling salted water for 6 minutes. Add 2 bunches of watercress and continue boiling for 5 minutes. Drain and put through a Mouli or liquidizer. Make ½ pint of Béchamel sauce (see page 119) and fold it into the purée, then add the cream. Season well.

This can be made in advance and reheated.

## CHOCOLATE CREAM PIE

PASTRY
125 g    *4 oz butter*
175 g    *6 oz plain flour*
35 g    *1½ oz ground almonds*
35 g    *1½ oz castor sugar*
*1 egg yolk*
*1 tablespoon cold water*

Mix the ingredients together till they look like breadcrumbs, mix in the egg and a little water till it forms a dough. Line an 8-inch (20-cm) flan dish or tin and bake blind for 15-20 minutes in a hot oven, 400°F 200°C gas 6. Cool.

FILLING
275 ml    *½ pint milk*
*1½ tablespoons cocoa*
*1 tablespoon sugar*
*1 tablespoon flour*
*1 tablespoon cornflour*
*2 beaten eggs*
25 g    *1 oz unsalted butter*
*2 teaspoons brandy*
175 g    *6 oz good black chocolate*
275 ml    *½ pint double cream*
25 g    *1 oz flaked toasted almonds*

Heat the milk, blend in the cocoa, sugar, flour and eggs. Blend the cornflour with a little milk and add to the mixture. Stir until thick over a low heat. Remove from the heat and stir in the butter, brandy and 4 oz of broken chocolate. Cool and pour into the flan case. Whip the cream and pile on to the top of the pie, grate the rest of the chocolate and sprinkle over the cream and top with almonds. Keep in the fridge.

This should be made in the morning or the day before so that it has time to cool.

PREPARATION TIME 30 minutes.

# Sunday Lunch

## (for 6 people)

### ROAST PORK

| | |
|---|---|
| 2½ kg | *1 small leg of pork about 5 lb* |

**SPICES**

*1 teaspoon salt*
*1 teaspoon black peppercorns, ground*
*1 crumbled bay leaf*
*Nutmeg, ground*
*Cloves, ground*

**MARINADE**

*2 medium sliced onions*
*4–5 thinly sliced garlic cloves*
*1 bottle cheap red wine*
150 ml *¼ pint olive oil*
275 ml *½ pint chicken stock*

This must be started at least 4 days before you need it.

Score the fat on the pork and rub in the mixture of spices. Keep for a day in the fridge. Remove from the fridge, put into a deep bowl surrounded with the onion and garlic, then pour in the liquids. Put back in the fridge and leave in the marinade for 3–4 days, turning the meat from time to time.

TO COOK dry the meat and keep the marinade. Rub the skin with olive oil and ground black pepper, put the joint on a rack in a roasting pan and cook in preheated oven, 325°F 170°C gas 3, for 25 minutes to the lb (500 g). Reduce the marinade to a third, adjust the seasoning, strain and serve with the meat.

**BAKED APPLES**

*6 small cooking apples*
*6 teaspoons crab apple jelly*

Core the apples and score round the middles. Cook in a baking tin in a little water until soft, but not collapsed – about 20 minutes. Fill the centres with crab apple jelly just before serving.

Sometimes I use little pastry boats instead of apple, but not when followed by treacle tart as here.

**ROAST POTATOES**

*3 medium-sized potatoes per person*

I par-boil the potatoes and then scratch with a fork to give a crisp surface before cooking in hot fat at the top of a hot oven.

# Sunday Lunch

### continued

## TREACLE TART

**PASTRY**

225 g  *8 oz plain flour*
*1 tablespoon icing sugar*
*Grated rind of ½ lemon*
*Squeeze of lemon juice*
*½ teaspoon salt*
125 g  *4 oz butter*
*1 egg yolk*

**FILLING**

*9 tablespoons golden syrup*
*2 tablespoons marmalade*
*2 tablespoons lemon juice*
*7 tablespoons white breadcrumbs*
*Grated rind of ½ lemon*

Make the pastry (see page 50)*

In a bowl mix the syrup, marmalade, lemon juice and breadcrumbs.* Spread the mixture in the pastry case and grate the lemon rind over the top. Decorate with a lattice of pastry strips made from the trimmings of the pastry and bake in the oven at 400°F 200°C gas 6 for 30 minutes.

*This can be prepared a day in advance.

# Sunday Supper

## (for 2 people)

### MUSHROOM AND MUSTARD SOUP

| | |
|---|---|
| 225 g | *8 oz sliced mushrooms* |
| 35 g | *1½ oz butter* |
| 275 ml | *½ pint chicken stock* |
| | *1½ tablespoons sherry* |
| 150 ml | *¼ pint double cream* |
| | *½ tablespoon French mustard* |

Cook the mushrooms in the butter for a few minutes. Add the chicken stock and sherry. Bring to the boil and add the French mustard. Put through a Mouli or liquidizer, add the cream, season and heat through gently.

### QUICK HOT BREAD

| | |
|---|---|
| | *1 packet bread mix* |
| 125 g | *4 oz strong Cheddar, grated* |
| | *1 teaspoon mustard powder* |

Make up the bread, following the instructions, but adding the cheese and mustard.

### COLD PORK

Slice the cold pork from lunch and serve with potatoes rolled in olive oil and salt, and baked in a hot oven for 1 hour.

### RED CABBAGE SALAD

| | |
|---|---|
| | *¼ red cabbage, sliced* |
| 50 g | *2 oz Roquefort* |
| 50 g | *2 oz walnuts* |
| | *2 tablespoons olive oil* |
| | *Juice of ½ lemon* |
| | *1½ tablespoons chopped parsley* |
| | *Salt and pepper* |

Mix the Roquefort with the cabbage. In a mixer blend the rest of the ingredients and pour over the salad. This dressing cannot be made too far in advance because the walnuts would make it go black.

# MARCH

## Sally Wigram

*Horris Farm was built at the
end of the seventeenth century and was
originally two farm cottages.
It has very pretty reddish pink brick,
a few thick beams, a mass of
small rooms, and 'an immensely cosy and
friendly atmosphere'.*

Sally pares her weekend cooking down to a minimum – for several reasons. First, she lives in London and commutes to the country for the weekend; and as she is unable to leave London before 4.30 p.m., when her daughters get out of school, she often arrives at the cottage only minutes before her visitors. Secondly, because she is very conscious of weight, and has teenage children who eat large quantities of anything, she prefers them to eat salads or fruit and not rich puddings. And thirdly, she would much rather spend the weekend playing tennis or weeding the garden than cooking. But her food is always simple and excellent.

'I nearly always cook the Friday night supper in London. This can be done on Thursday when I shop, or on Friday morning; because I am in London I shop there and take supplies down to the country with me. I cook well-tried recipes that I know will take only a few moments.'

On weekend mornings Sally's table is always laid for breakfast with fruit, cereal, toast and marmalade. She prefers to leave people to get what they want, when they want it, which means they can appear at any hour and sit for as long as they want over the newspapers and a cup of coffee. But as a special favour on Saturdays she may grill some tomatoes and bacon.

'On Saturday morning I make a huge quantity of vinaigrette for salads, and chop parsley. I also rely on really good brown bread to go with most meals. Everything else on my menus can be done very simply at the last minute. The avocado and tomato starter for Saturday is unbelievably delicious – I was very reluctant to give the recipe – and very simple to prepare.'

Sally's wine list at the cottage is also very simple; the white wine is Wheeler's *vin de table* and the red is Club Claret, both bought from her local branch of Augustus Barnet, a large chain of wine merchants which Sally thinks produces really good quality wines at reasonable prices. On special occasions when her brother-in-law is staying at the cottage he opens some 1945 Beychevelle, a red Bordeaux which is 'quite fantastic'.

## Friday

**SUPPER**

Oxtail Stew
Salad
Brown Bread

## Saturday

**LUNCH**

Cottage Pie and Tomato Sauce
Cabbage

Cheddar
Fruit

**DINNER**

Tomato, Avocado, Smoked Salmon and Egg Starter

Grilled Poussin and White Wine Sauce
Courgettes
Brown Rice

Cheese and Fruit

## Sunday

**LUNCH**

Leg of Lamb
Potatoes, Onions and Cream
Cauliflower
Peas

Apple Meringue

**SUPPER** (in London)

Scrambled Eggs and Bacon

# Friday Supper

(for 6 people)

---

## OXTAIL STEW

*1 large oxtail*
*1 medium-sized tin of
    tomato juice*
*1 large onion*
100 g *4 oz mushrooms*
*1 tin of petit pois*
*1 glass white wine*
*Oil and margarine*
*2 tablespoons plain flour*
*Bay leaves*
*Chicken stock cube*
*Seasoning*
*Tabasco*
*Parsley*

This needs to be made well in advance because oxtail is extremely fatty and the stew has to cool and be skimmed. I would cook this on Thursday, skim it and add the vegetables and wine on Friday morning, and heat it up at the cottage on arrival.

Chop onion and fry slowly in a heavy casserole in 2 tablespoons of oil and a knob of margarine. Trim fat off oxtail pieces, coat them well with flour and brown them with the onion. Sprinkle a tablespoon of flour over the meat and when absorbed add enough tomato juice to cover. Add stock cube, salt, black pepper, a good dash of Tabasco and 2 bay leaves. Cover the casserole.

When the stew begins to bubble gently place it in the oven for 3–4 hours at 300°F 150°C gas 2. Cool and skim thoroughly.

Just before serving, add the chopped mushrooms, petit pois and the white wine. Eat with delicious brown bread and a green salad.

PREPARATION TIME 30 minutes.

Serve with a large bowl of salad and vinaigrette.

**VINAIGRETTE**

*3 tablespoons Mazola oil*
*½ tablespoon malt vinegar*
*½ tablespoon wine vinegar*
*1 teaspoon English mustard*
*A dash of Tabasco*
*A dash of Maggi sauce*
*1 clove of garlic*
*Salt and pepper*

Put the mustard into a large bowl or jug and add the oil, vinegar, Tabasco, Maggi sauce, salt and black pepper. Take a wire whisk and whisk really well. Put a clove of garlic in the bottom of a glass jar or bottle and pour the vinaigrette on top. You can add more oil and vinegar to make a larger amount and this keeps well for 3–4 weeks.

---

# Saturday Lunch

## (for 6 people)

### COTTAGE PIE

750 g  *1½ lb mince*
       *6 large potatoes*
       *1 tablespoon flour*
       *1 large onion*
125 ml *¼ pint tomato juice*
       *2 tablespoons margarine*
       *Seasoning*
       *Tabasco*

Peel potatoes, boil them and mash thoroughly, adding margarine, milk, salt and pepper.

Fry the chopped onion in a little margarine and add the mince, shaking a tablespoon of flour over it all. Mix together the onion and mince and enough tomato juice to moisten the meat. Add salt, pepper and Tabasco to taste. Put the meat in an ovenproof dish and *when cool* put the mashed potato on top.* Reheat in a hot oven for 20 minutes.

PREPARATION TIME 30 minutes.

*Can be made up to 2 days in advance.

Eat with carrots, cooked in boiling salted water for 5 minutes, and white cabbage, cooked for 4 minutes – both under-done and crunchy.

Follow with Farmhouse Cheddar and apples.

MARCH

# Saturday Dinner

## (for 8 people)

### SMOKED SALMON STARTER

8 hard-boiled eggs, finely
   chopped
250 g   8 oz smoked salmon, cut
   into thin strips
8 tomatoes, peeled and
   sliced
2 avocado pears, sliced
1 tablespoon of chopped
   onion and parsley
Vinaigrette

Put the chopped egg on the bottom of a large serving plate. Cover with the thin strips of smoked salmon, then the slices of avocado, and top it with sliced tomatoes. Sprinkle chopped onion and parsley all over the top and just before serving pour 6 tablespoons of strong lemony vinaigrette over it all. Serve with brown bread and butter.

PREPARATION TIME 30 minutes.

### GRILLED POUSSIN AND WHITE WINE SAUCE

4 poussins
2–3 glasses white wine
3 tablespoons double cream
1 chicken stock cube
1 tablespoon plain flour
Maggi sauce
Fresh rosemary
Salt and pepper
1 tablespoon parsley
   or chives, chopped

Cut each poussin in half and place them in a grill pan with butter, Maggi sauce, salt, pepper and fresh rosemary. Cook under a high grill for 10 minutes on each side. Remove poussins and place them in a large shallow dish.

   With the juices left in the grill pan make a sauce by adding a tablespoon of the flour, blending it thoroughly, and adding a chicken stock cube, 2–3 glasses of white wine and 3 tablespoons of double cream. Pour this over the poussins and top with chopped chives and parsley.

PREPARATION TIME 45 minutes.

Serve with brown rice; and courgettes, sliced and boiled for 2 minutes.

Follow with Brie and biscuits.

# Sunday Lunch

## (for 6 people)

---

### ROAST LEG OF LAMB

2 kg    *4½–5 lb leg of lamb*
*1 clove garlic*
*Rosemary*
*Salt and pepper*
*1 tablespoon plain flour*
*1 chicken stock cube*
*Gravy browning*
*Dash of white wine*

Preheat oven to 450°F 230°C gas 8. Cut the garlic clove in 3 and insert the pieces in the skin of the lamb. Rub in some coarse salt and sprinkle the top with black pepper and rosemary. Place the lamb in a hot oven and cook for 15 minutes, then turn the oven down to 350°F 180°C gas 4 for a further 1¼ hours. Put the lamb on a meat board for serving.

Having removed the excess fat from the roasting pan, blend in a tablespoon of flour, add a chicken stock cube, gravy browning, ½ pint (275 ml) of water or stock and a dash of white wine.

### POTATOES IN CREAM

*8 large potatoes*
*2 onions*
275 ml    *½ pint single cream*
*Salt and pepper*

Peel and slice the potatoes and onions. Butter an ovenproof dish and put the potatoes and onions in layers with salt and pepper over each layer. Pour ½ pint (275 ml) of single cream over the top and bake in the oven at 350°F 180°C gas 4 for 1 hour.

**PREPARATION TIME** 45 minutes.

Serve the lamb and potatoes together with a large cauliflower, cooked in boiling salted water for just 4 minutes.

### APPLE MERINGUE

*4 large Bramley apples*
*Brown sugar*
150 g    *6 oz white sugar*
*3 egg whites*

Cook the peeled, cored and sliced apples in a little water with brown sugar for about 7 minutes. Drain and transfer them to a suitable baking dish. Whisk the egg whites, adding half the sugar half way through whisking, the rest at the end. Pour the mixture on top of the apple and cook for 2 hours in a very low oven, 225°F 110°C gas ¼.

**PREPARATION TIME** 30 minutes    **COOKING TIME** 2 hours.

# Sunday Supper

## (in London, for 4 people)

Scrambled eggs and bacon

---

# Angela Huth

Perched on a hill, almost in the centre of Oxford, is Angela's glorious turreted Victorian house, surrounded by a huge tangled garden.

'I am by nature a reluctant cook. I am also very anxious that our guests should eat well, and therein the conflict. But for the most part I become enthusiastic at the thought of cooking for a whole weekend of visitors, and only slip back to the reluctant state on Sunday night (by which time all decent and considerate guests should have left).

'As one who has no talent for spontaneous spaghetti, I appreciate a lot of advance warning. The constant drain on the deep freeze during the week means it is never full of things I should be able to fall back upon. If in March it is arranged people will be coming in May, I do the dotty thing of planning the menu immediately, so *that* burden should be off my mind, and I do not have to think about it again until a few days beforehand. If the menu includes new things, I experiment on the family, who are quite fierce in their criticisms. Thus gradually the list of old favourites increases, and I try to remember that although we have had Greek lamb five hundred times, it may be a new delight to others.

'I am convinced it is quite in order to foist upon my friends the kind of food I like myself, and therefore cook best. So in our house you will never find beef hiding under a bushel of pastry, or intricate sauces that raise the nervous tension and keep me away from the fun. But you will find a great many puddings, which I love, and so in fact do most people who boast they never eat them. For Saturday lunch, visitors will often have to endure my particular delight of *two* first courses, and a pudding, and if they are plainly reliable guests – i.e. guaranteed to dash to the table when called – they may be rewarded by one of my hundred best soufflés.

'My method of organization is simple: for a start my morning expression is designed not to encourage cooked breakfast, but under pressure I will rise to a boiled egg. About once a year, should we be lucky enough to have been asked out to Sunday lunch, I will lash out with Haddock Kedgeree, and for especially endearing guests I will even squeeze real orange juice. But apart from masses of cereal, there is always home-made brown bread for toast, home-made marmalade and High Dumpsie Dearie jam – the best jam in the world – from Edith's Café in Marlborough.

'I do everything possible in advance so that only the most discerning guest will guess at the amazing efforts that have gone on behind the scenes. When I lived in Wiltshire shopping was very easy in the marvellous town of Marlborough. Now, still unaccustomed to the outrageous prices and inferior quality of city produce, I continue to find it cheaper and less frustrating to return to Marlborough for the Wednesday market. I begin to cook on Thursday and Friday, think of Saturday night as the big effort of the weekend, and try to plan a relatively simple Sunday lunch. But there are many things that cannot be done in advance, and in order to spend as much time as possible with the guests the only answer is secret preparation at dawn.

'I do not encourage kind help. On the whole it is a hindrance. A brilliant academic can take ten minutes to find a wooden spoon, the finest mind cannot be expected to know my special way of stacking the dishwasher. No, guests can be most useful by going away. All I ask – and am fortunate in getting – is aid from husband and daughter, who know without asking.

'The art of a relaxed weekend is merely an enormous amount of unobserved work, but it is worth it when you consider that soon it will be your turn, and in someone else's house the wonderful food and roses in every corner will be doubly appreciated, when you know precisely what labours of love have been exercised to produce them.'

## Friday

Baked Pork Chops in Orange
Baked Potatoes

Watercress Salad and Cheese

## Saturday

LUNCH

Smoked Mackerel Kedgeree with Brown Rice
Raw Spinach and Avocado Salad

Marmalade Biscuit Fool

DINNER

Snaffles Starter

Sesame Chicken
Mashed Potatoes
Baked Leeks

Mulberry Clafoutis

## Sunday

LUNCH

Greek Lamb
Pureé of Celeriac
Pan-Stirred Carrots

Sussex Pond Pudding

# Friday Supper

## (for 6 people)

### BAKED PORK CHOPS IN ORANGE

*12 thin pork chops*
150 g *1 container of frozen orange juice (about 5 fl oz)*
272 ml *½ pint good dry cider*
*Fresh rosemary*
*Seasoning*

Trim the fat from the chops and arrange them overlapping in a shallow dish. Dot with lumps of frozen orange juice (about half the container) and pour over enough cider almost to cover the chops. Season, sprinkle generously with fresh rosemary.* Bake in a moderate oven at 350°F 180°C gas 4 for ¾ hour, turning up heat at the end to brown. They can survive in a warm oven for an hour or so if necessary. Serve with baked potatoes followed by watercress salad and cheese.

PREPARATION TIME 10 minutes.

*Can be prepared in the morning.

MARCH

# Saturday Lunch

## (for 6 people)

### SMOKED MACKEREL KEDGEREE WITH BROWN RICE

|  |  |
|---|---|
|  | 6 small or 4 large smoked mackerel fillets |
| 225 g | 8 oz brown rice |
|  | 6 eggs |
|  | Freshly chopped parsley |
|  | Seasoning |
| 150 ml | ¼ pint cream (optional) |
| 35 g | 1½ oz butter (optional) |

Cook the rice until *al dente* – about 25 minutes. Scrape skins from fish and roughly chop. Hard-boil the eggs and chop. Combine rice, fish, eggs and seasoning.

The oiliness of the fish makes butter unnecessary, but for a richer version add butter and hot cream at the last minute. Decorate with a little chopped parsley.

PREPARATION TIME 30 minutes.

### RAW SPINACH AND AVOCADO SALAD

|  |  |
|---|---|
| 350 g | 12 oz fresh young spinach |
|  | 2 avocado pears |

Wash and finely shred the spinach. Slice the avocados. Toss both in a French dressing made with an extra amount of Dijon mustard.

### MARMALADE BISCUIT FOOL

|  |  |
|---|---|
|  | 6 cooking apples |
|  | 2 tablespoons demerara sugar |
|  | Cinnamon |
|  | Grated peel of 1 orange |
|  | 4 tablespoons coarse-cut marmalade |
| 150 ml | 1 5-fluid oz carton natural yogurt |
| 100 g | 4 oz crushed digestive biscuits |

Peel, core and slice the apples; stew with the brown sugar, cinnamon and a little water till soft – about 7 minutes. Take off heat and add the grated orange peel, marmalade and yogurt. Put all in the blender and whizz till smooth. Chill.*

Serve cold, topped with a crust of crushed digestive biscuits added at the last minute.

PREPARATION TIME 15 minutes.

*This much can be done in advance.

# Saturday Dinner

## (for 8 people)

---

### SNAFFLES STARTER

450 ml    *16 oz Philadephia*
            *cream cheese*
2 × 270 g   *2 × 10½ oz tins of beef*
            *consommé*
     *1 small clove of garlic,*
        *crushed*
     *1 teaspoon curry powder*
     *Dash of sherry*
     *Seasoning*
     *Parsley and lemon wedges for*
        *garnishing*

I first ate this in the famous Snaffles Restaurant in Dublin. It can be made well in advance and nobody ever seems to be able to guess what it is.

Blend all the ingredients in a liquidizer. Put into individual ramekins and chill till set. Garnish with chopped parsley and lemon wedges. Serve with hot toast.

     Can be made a day in advance.

PREPARATION TIME 5 minutes.

### SESAME CHICKEN

*8–10 chicken breasts*
     *(or thighs)*
*1 tablespoon butter*
*1 tablespoon olive oil*
*Sesame seeds*
*A good quantity of*
     *dry cider*
*Parsley*
*1 large onion*
*Seasoning*

Finely chop the onion. In a casserole dish melt the butter and oil and lightly brown the chicken breasts. Put to one side and fry the onion until just soft. Put back the chicken breasts, season with coarse salt and freshly milled pepper. Scatter quite thickly with sesame seeds (toast in a hot oven for a few moments if they are pale). Pour over enough cider to cover the chicken breasts.*

     Cover and bake in a medium oven, 350°F 180°C gas 4, for 1 hour. Sprinkle with chopped parsley and serve in the casserole dish.

PREPARATION TIME 15 minutes.

*All this can be done several hours in advance.

Serve with mashed potatoes beaten with one egg, nutmeg, and an extravagant amount of cream.

### BAKED LEEKS

*1 large leek or 2 small ones*
     *per person*
*Butter*
*Seasoning*

Grease a shallow dish. Peel the outer layers from the leeks and wash well. Cut into large matchstick slices and arrange in the dish. Dot with butter and season. Cover dish tightly with tin foil.*

     Cook in the medium oven, 350°F 180°C gas 4, for approximately 1 hour.

*Can be prepared to this point well in advance.

---

### MULBERRY CLAFOUTIS

¾–1 kg    *1½–2 lb of fruit*
*A little castor sugar*
*Whipped cream*

BATTER

2 × 150 ml    *2 × 5 fl oz cartons*
*sour cream*
*2 tablespoons sugar*
*2 tablespoons plain flour*
*2 eggs*

If you are lucky enough to have a mulberry tree this is the nicest way I know of eating the fruit. Frozen mulberries are equally good, or frozen raspberries; even tinned black unsweetened cherries are an excellent substitute.

The batter can be mixed in advance. Whisk up the ingredients till smooth; if the batter looks too thick to cover the fruit, thin with a little milk.

Put the mulberries (or whatever fruit you are using) into a shallow dish. If they are frozen and produce a lot of juice, throw at least half of it away. Pour the batter over the fruit and bake in a low oven, 200°F 100°C gas 2, for 45 minutes. Turn up the heat for a further 10 minutes to 300°F 150°C gas 4 or until the batter is bubbling and browned.
   Sprinkle with castor sugar and serve with whipped cream.

PREPARATION TIME 10 minutes.

# Sunday Lunch
## (for 6 people)

### GREEK LAMB

| | |
|---|---|
| $1\frac{3}{4}$–$2\frac{1}{4}$ kg | *4–5 lb leg of lamb* |
| 100 g | *4 oz thick honey* |
| | *Ground ginger* |
| 275 ml | *$\frac{1}{2}$ pint good dry cider* |
| | *Fresh rosemary* |
| | *Seasoning* |

New Zealand lamb is fine for this recipe. Put the joint in roasting tin, spread all over with honey, season with salt and pepper, then a generous amount of ground ginger. Stick twigs of fresh rosemary all over the joint and pour the cider into the pan. Roast in a hot oven, 400°F 200°C gas 6 for 20 minutes per pound, basting frequently. Add more cider if necessary towards the end of the cooking. Combined with the honey and meat juices it makes a most delicious gravy.

Serve with roast potatoes (see page 31).

### PUREE OF CELERIAC

| | |
|---|---|
| | *2 whole celeriac roots* |
| | *Butter* |
| 75 ml | *$\frac{1}{8}$ pint single cream* |
| | *Seasoning* |

Peel and chop the celeriac into smallish pieces. Boil in salted water till soft. Drain thoroughly and liquidize till quite smooth. Return to the saucepan, add the butter, seasoning and cream; heat through. This will keep quite happily warm in the oven, in a dish covered with tin foil.

### PAN-STIRRED CARROTS

| | |
|---|---|
| 750 g | *$1\frac{1}{2}$ lb carrots* |
| | *Sugar* |
| | *Seasoning* |
| | *Squeeze of lemon* |
| | *A little cream (optional)* |

Wash and peel the carrots, then grate or shred finely in a food processor. At the last possible moment heat a small amount of butter in a saucepan, throw in the carrots, season with salt, pepper, sugar to taste and a squeeze of lemon. Quickly stir till carrots are heated through, but stop before they become soggy. Add a little cream if you like and garnish with chopped parsley.

### SUSSEX POND PUDDING

225 g   *8 oz self-raising flour*
100 g   *4 oz chopped suet*
100 g   *4 oz butter*
150 ml  *Scant ¼ pint milk and
        water (mixed)*
100 g   *4 oz demerara sugar
        4 lemons*

Of all the English suet puddings this is the best I know. In this recipe it is made with lemons, but it is also very good made with rhubarb.

Mix the flour and suet together. Make into a dough with milk and water. Roll out the suet, remove one third and reserve for the lid. Grease a 2–2½ pint (1 litre) pudding basin well and line with the suet pastry. Chop the butter into small pieces, put half into the base of the basin. Add half the sugar. Cut the lemons into quarters (into eighths if the lemons are very large), seed them and lay them on top. Cover with the rest of the chopped butter and sugar. Roll out the suet lid. Lay it on top of the filling and press down firmly so that the pudding is completely sealed.*

Cover the basin with an oiled piece of greaseproof paper, then a piece of tin foil; secure with string and make a handle. Put into a pan of boiling water which comes half way up the basin. Cover and boil for 3½–4 hours. Add more boiling water if necessary: the water must retain its height.

TO SERVE remove the paper and turn the pudding out gently into a shallow dish. The sugary brown sauce will escape from the suet – thus the name pond – and the lemons will have disintegrated tartly into the sweet sauce. Serve with thick cream.

PREPARATION TIME 20 minutes.

*This can be prepared a day in advance.

*Angela Huth's house was built*
*in 1883 and is a mile from the centre of Oxford*

# APRIL

## Angela Huth

## Friday

**SUPPER**

Eggs in Gruyère Cheese Sauce
Baked Potatoes
Green Salad

Yogurt Cream Pudding

## Saturday

**LUNCH**

Millionaires Hamburgers
White Cabbage and Dill

Apple Toffee Pudding

**DINNER**

Curried Melon

Green Chicken
Baked Courgettes
Brown Rice

Crème Brulée Ice Cream

## Sunday

**LUNCH**

Durham Lamb Squab Pie
Cauliflower with Pea Sauce

Lemon Pudding

**SUPPER**

Haddock and Dill Soufflé
Tomatoes Baked with Fresh Breadcrumbs

# Friday Supper

## (for 6 people)

### EGGS IN GRUYERE CHEESE SAUCE

12 eggs
575 ml  1 pint milk
        2 tablespoons plain flour
        4 tablespoons butter
50 g    2 oz Cheddar
225 g   8 oz Gruyère
        2 Spanish onions
        6 tablespoons fresh
          breadcrumbs
        Dijon mustard
        Salt and pepper

Hard-boil the eggs. Peel and slice the onions and fry in 2 tablespoons butter until soft, but not brown. Melt the rest of the butter in a saucepan and add the flour off the heat. Add the milk. When thick add the grated Cheddar, mustard and seasoning.

Slice the hard-boiled eggs in half and lay them flat side down in a large shallow dish. Cover with onions, then the cheese sauce,* and bake in a moderate oven, 350°F 180°C gas 4 for ¼ hour.

Spoon over the cream, sprinkle the grated Gruyère and top with breadcrumbs. Put under the grill until the breadcrumbs are toasted.

*This much can be done in advance: continue with the recipe 20 minutes before you want it.

Serve with baked potatoes (see page 28) and a green salad.

### YOGURT CREAM PUDDING

275 ml  ½ pint double cream
575 ml  1 pint natural yogurt
        2 lemons
        Soft brown sugar

Whip the cream, fold in the yogurt. Grate the rind of the lemons and mix in. Put into a dish and cover with a thick layer of brown sugar. Refrigerate for 2 hours, by which time the sugar will have melted.

# Saturday Lunch

(for 6 people)

## MILLIONAIRES HAMBURGERS

| | |
|---|---|
| 1 kg | *2 lb minced beef* |
| | *1 egg* |
| | *Tabasco* |
| | *Worcester sauce* |
| | *5 cooked beetroot* |
| 150 ml | *¼ pint double cream* |
| | *Salt and pepper* |

I cook these hamburgers as each person wants them. They only take a few moments and are the best variation on a hamburger I know. They were devised by that famous cook Mrs Eaton, better known as Edgy.

Chop the beetroot very fine indeed or put through a food processor. In a very large bowl mix the meat, beetroot and all the other ingredients. Divide into separate hamburgers about 4 oz (100 g) each.*

Roll the hamburgers lightly in flour and either grill under a hot flame (so that they are burnt on the outside and rare inside), or – preferable I think – cook on a cast-iron steak griddle.

*Can be prepared in advance to this stage.

### WHITE CABBAGE AND DILL

*1 white cabbage*
*Dill weed*
*Butter*

I never boil cabbage, always steam. It is particularly good cooked with dill weed (not the seed).

Chop the cabbage and put in a steamer on top of a saucepan of boiling water. Season and add a good scattering of dill weed. Cook for about 6–7 minutes: the cabbage should still be crisp and scarcely done. Drain thoroughly, toss with butter and serve at once.

## APPLE TOFFEE PUDDING

| | |
|---|---|
| 50 g | *2 oz suet* |
| 100 g | *4 oz self-raising flour* |
| | *1 scantly rounded teaspoon baking powder* |
| | *Cold water* |
| | *Golden syrup* |
| | *Brown sugar* |
| 350 g | *12 oz cooking apples, peeled and cored* |
| | *Lemon juice* |

Mix the suet, flour and baking powder well. Bind to a stiff dough with cold water. Cut off 3 oz (75 g) suet and roll the remainder. Oil an 8-inch (20-cm) flan dish and line with suet. Lay thinly sliced apples in three layers, giving each layer a squeeze of lemon juice and a sprinkling of brown sugar. Roll out the remaining suet thinly and cover the top completely. Press down firmly and cover liberally with golden syrup and brown sugar. Bake at 350°F 180°C gas 4 for 40 minutes or until crustily brown on top. Be sure to put an oven dish under the pie as the sauce will trickle over the sides. Serve with thick cream.

PREPARATION TIME 15 minutes.

# Saturday Dinner

## (for 8 people)

### CURRIED MELON

*1 large cantaloup melon*
*1 cucumber*
*1 heaped teaspoon*
*curry powder*
*Juice of 1 lemon*
*4 tablespoons olive oil*
*Salt and pepper*

Cut the melon in half and de-seed; cut out the flesh and dice quite small. Peel and dice the cucumber, mix the two together, season to taste. Heat the lemon juice, oil and curry powder over a low flame, stirring continuously until well mixed. Cool and pour over the melon and cucumber. Mix well and put into individual ramekins and chill for a couple of hours. Sprinkle with a little chopped parsley or paprika.

PREPARATION TIME 10 minutes.

### GREEN CHICKEN

*8 chicken breasts*
*1 green pepper*
*1 cucumber*
*1 tablespoon butter*
*1 tablespoon olive oil*
275 ml *½ pint good dry cider*
*1 large handful of mint*
*leaves*
*Salt and freshly ground*
*pepper*
*Crushed garlic (optional)*

Melt the butter and oil in a large casserole dish and brown the chicken; add a crushed clove of garlic if you like. Peel and dice the cucumber, de-seed and chop the green pepper. Throw these over the chicken. Season. Add enough cider just to cover the chicken and add the mint leaves. Bake in a moderate oven, 375°F 190°C gas 5, for ¾ hour or until bubbling. Serve with brown rice.

PREPARATION TIME 20 minutes.

### BAKED COURGETTES

*3 small courgettes*
*per person*
*Butter*
*Seasoning*

Grease a shallow fireproof dish. Wash courgettes and slice very thinly either by hand or in a food processor. Arrange in overlapping rows in a dish; season well with sea salt and freshly ground black pepper. Dot with butter, cover tightly with foil and bake in a moderate oven, 375°F 190°C gas 5, for ¾ hour.

PREPARATION TIME 7 minutes.

### CREME BRULEE ICE CREAM

This amazingly rich and delicious ice cream can be made any amount of time ahead and kept in the deep freeze.

*8 large egg yolks*
725 ml *1¼ pints double cream*
275 g *10 oz granulated sugar*
*Vanilla essence*

Beat egg yolks with 4 oz (100 g) of sugar and a few drops of vanilla essence. Put the cream into a double saucepan and scald. Do not boil. Pour cream on to egg mixture and beat again. Pour back into saucepan and stir continuously, making sure the water in the double saucepan is simmering, not boiling.

As soon as the cream mixture is the consistency of a thickish custard take the saucepan off the heat and plunge it into a sink of cold water to prevent further cooking. It is essential not to let the mixture boil or it will curdle and be ruined – take it off the heat too early rather than too late. When cool pour into container and put, covered, into deep freeze.

In a heavy saucepan heat 6 oz (175 g) sugar and 2–3 tablespoons of water. Boil hard until the syrup is a good golden colour. Put into a large flat baking tin, moving it about until it forms a very thin sheet of caramel. When quite cold and hard put it in a plastic bag and bash it with a hammer until it is broken into fragments. After two hours in the deep freeze remove the cream custard, stir up well with a fork, mix in the caramel chips and make sure they don't all go to the bottom. Seal tightly and return to the deep freeze until ready to serve.

PREPARATION TIME 30 minutes.

# Sunday Lunch
## (for 6 people)

### DURHAM LAMB SQUAB PIE

6 large lamb chops or
  12 good cutlets
3 cooking apples, peeled
  and sliced
1 large onion, peeled and
  chopped
Seasoning
2 teaspoons brown sugar
275 ml  ½ pint chicken stock
1 kg  2 lb potatoes

Peel and thinly slice potatoes and cover with cold salted water. Fry well-trimmed chops in butter until the juices begin to run. Transfer to a plate. In the remaining butter gently fry the apples and onions. Drain the potatoes and cover the bottom of a shallow greased ovenproof dish with half of them. Lay the chops on top, season and spoon over the apple and onion mixture. Sprinkle with 2 teaspoons of brown sugar. Cover with the rest of the potatoes, season again and pour over the chicken stock. Brush the potatoes with melted butter and cook in a moderate oven, 350°F 180°C gas 4, for 1 hour. Garnish with chopped parsley.

PREPARATION TIME 20 minutes.

### CAULIFLOWER WITH PEA SAUCE

1 large cauliflower
275 g  10 oz packet frozen
  petit pois
3 tablespoons single cream
Seasoning

Put the cauliflower in boiling salted water and cook for 6–7 minutes. Cook the peas, following the instructions on the packet. Purée the peas, add the cream and check the seasoning. Place the cauliflower on a serving dish. Pour over the pea purée and serve. This can be kept hot for about ½ hour.

### LEMON PUDDING

The delight of this pudding is that under the fluffy sponge you find the lemon sauce.

40 g  1½ oz butter
175 g  6 oz sugar
4 eggs, separated
2 lemons
4 tablespoons plain flour
2 cups of milk

Cream together the butter and sugar till fluffy. In another bowl mix the flour, egg yolks, milk, grated rind and juice of lemons. Fold this into the sugar and butter mixture. Beat the egg whites until stiff and fold them in lightly. Pour into a buttered soufflé dish and bake in a *bain marie* in a fairly hot oven, 400°F 200°C gas 6, for about ½ hour. Serve with cream.

# Friday Supper

(for 2–4 people)

## HADDOCK AND DILL SOUFFLE

500 g    *1 lb smoked haddock*
        *(Finnan or fillets)*
       *6 eggs, separated*
       *1 rounded tablespoon flour*
       *1 rounded tablespoon butter*
425 ml   *¾ pint milk*
       *Good handful of dill weed,*
        *chopped*

Bake haddock fillets in a hot oven, covered with milk, for about 10 minutes. When cooked scrape flesh from skin and mash well. Retain the milk and make an ordinary roux from the butter and flour and add the milk. When it has cooked for a few moments remove from the heat and add the egg yolks, beating in each one well. Add salt, pepper and a good handful of dill weed. Stir in mashed haddock. Beat the egg whites stiffly and fold gently into the haddock mixture with a metal spoon. Transfer to a greased soufflé dish and bake in a hottish oven, 400°F 200°C gas 6, for 25 minutes. Do not over-cook; the soufflé should have a slightly runny middle.

PREPARATION TIME 20 minutes

Prepare these before the soufflé so they can cook together.

## TOMATOES BAKED WITH BREADCRUMBS

*4 large tomatoes*
*1 large handful*
  *fresh breadcrumbs*
*Mixed herbs*
*Butter*
*Seasoning*

Cut the tomatoes in half and lay in a greased shallow ovenproof dish. Season with salt and pepper and a small amount of mixed dried herbs. Sprinkle with breadcrumbs, dot with butter and bake in a hottish oven, 400°F 200°C gas 6, for 25 minutes.

# Noni de Zoete

The small village of Colemore is approached by a very narrow lane and lies six hundred feet above sea level at the start of the Meon Valley in Hampshire. There is Noni's house, a small church originating from the twelfth century, a farm and four or five cottages. There are no shops or post office.

'Although I plan my menus early in the week, I rarely think about the weekend until it is upon me, then cook at least two recipes at the same time. I shop locally for most of my food; occasionally I may get the more unusual items from London and have a supply of fresh vegetables from the garden.

Having lived most of her life in Australia, Noni found the food in Europe 'more imaginative'. But, she says, she had learnt from her native country that presentation is important. 'On returning from my honeymoon, I discovered my husband had booked me into a cooking school immediately as I could hardly even boil an egg. For a while we had to eat the dish I had learnt that day since I didn't know anything else to cook. The first meal I served was a lemon soufflé and that was all.

'I always have in the fridge bowls of food like fresh breadcrumbs, grated cheese, stocks and mayonnaise. I prepare everything I can in advance and then assemble it at the last minute. My deep freeze is used mainly for children's meals – uncooked home-made hamburgers or mince cooked with onions ready for pies, and ice cream. I rarely have meat that needs carving, so serving is always quick, which is important with large numbers.

'Most of my food can be prepared a day or so in advance if one is organized – I always try to have at least one of the recipes for each meal cooked the day before.'

Noni always *offers* a proper cooked breakfast, and finds it usually accepted, especially on a Saturday morning. This might be sausages, bacon and eggs, and over the Christmas weekend a slice of ham with a poached or scrambled egg. On Sunday mornings however, she finds people prefer just a plain boiled egg. There is always fresh bread, home-made jam, and orange juice, and a large thermos of good coffee is kept filled all morning.

## Friday

**SUPPER**

Spinach Quiche

Chicken in Wine and Cheese Sauce
Boiled Potatoes
Green Beans

Lemon Chiffon

## Saturday

**LUNCH**

Crumbed Veal Cutlets
Green Salad

Orange Meringue Pudding

**DINNER**

Cod with Prawns and Olives

Loin of Pork with Wine and Herbs
Baked Apples
Glazed Carrots
Purée of Spinach

Chocolate Roulade

## Sunday

**LUNCH**

Leg of Lamb in Lemon and Garlic Crust
Roast Potatoes
Peas
Cauliflower

Rhubarb Crumble

**SUPPER**

Salad Soup

Potted Shrimps and Scrambled Eggs
Cheese

# Friday Supper

(for 6 people)

## SPINACH QUICHE

Combine flour and salt in bowl. Add butter, cut into small pieces, and mix until mixture resembles breadcrumbs, pinching with fingertips and lifting up to aerate. Add egg and water mixed all at once and mix with knife until a dough is formed. Alternatively process in Magimix, reducing water to 2 tablespoons.* Turn on to floured board and roll out. Press into a greased 8-inch (20-cm) flan tin, prick bottom lightly with fork. Cover pastry with foil and fill with dried beans. Bake blind at 375°F 190°C gas 5 for 10 minutes. Remove foil and beans and put back in oven for a further 4 minutes to dry out bottom of flan.

Soften shallots in butter, cook spinach and drain well, pressing out all excess moisture. Mix together. Beat eggs and cream together lightly, add spinach and season.* Put in flan case, sprinkle with cheese and cook at 375°F 190°C gas 5 for 30 minutes.

*Mix the pastry and the filling on Thursday and cook both at the last minute.

## CHICKEN IN WINE AND CHEESE SAUCE

This sauce is also excellent with fish, veal or pork.

Joint chicken and sauté gently in frying pan for 10–15 minutes, turning occasionally. Place in ovenproof dish.

Mix together tomato purée and wine, add cheese, salt and pepper and mix well. Whip cream lightly and add, stirring well. Pour sauce over chicken, cook in a hot oven, 400°F 200°C gas 6, for 15 minutes.

TO DECORATE skin tomato by plunging into boiling water, cut into quarters and remove pips, then cut into thin strips. Place on top of chicken and leave in oven to warm tomato for a few minutes.

Serve with boiled baby new potatoes: scrape and boil for 10 minutes, drain and add 1 oz butter, salt and pepper and a little chopped parsley or mint.

GREEN BEANS Plunge green beans into boiling salted water, cook for 6 minutes, drain and add $\frac{1}{2}$ oz (12$\frac{1}{2}$ g) butter, salt and pepper. The beans should be crisp and hot: it is better to undercook them, especially if they have to wait in the oven before serving.

# *Friday Supper*

## continued

### LEMON CHIFFON

1 round teaspoon gelatine
¼ cup warm water
2 lemons
4 eggs
100 g   4 oz castor sugar
Pinch salt
150 ml   ¼ pint double cream

Dissolve gelatine in water. Separate eggs. Grate, peel and juice lemons (if small warm slightly to extract more juice) and add to egg yolks and 2 oz of the sugar. Beat with a whisk over a double saucepan or in a bowl over a saucepan of very hot water until mixture thickens and is light and fluffy. Set aside to cool, whisking occasionally. Beat egg whites with salt until stiff, beat in rest of sugar. Fold half of whites into lemon mixture, add gelatine and then fold in rest of egg whites.* Chill. Decorate with extra lemon rind if desired or pipe with whipped cream. Serve with cream.

*Can be made on Thursday.

# Saturday Lunch

## (for 6 people)

---

## CRUMBED VEAL CUTLETS

*12 small veal cutlets or
6 chops*

I am able to get from my butcher small cutlets similar to best end of lamb cutlets, but the larger veal chops are also suitable. I prepare the crumb mixture in advance and keep it covered in the fridge, then I coat the cutlets just before frying.

CRUMB MIXTURE

*4 rounded tablespoons
grated mature Cheddar
2 rounded tablespoons
breadcrumbs
½ teaspoon salt and pepper
1 egg, lightly beaten*

Grate cheese finely, add breadcrumbs and salt and pepper. Place in wide bowl or soup plate. Trim cutlets, blot up excess moisture from meat, dip into beaten egg, place on crumb mixture and press crumbs firmly on all sides of cutlets.

Melt 2 oz (50 g) dripping or lard and fry cutlets gently for 5 minutes on each side. Place on serving dish and keep warm.

Serve with a green salad consisting of lettuce, cucumber, green pepper, sliced onion, watercress and sliced button mushrooms.

Make plenty of salad because what is left over will be used up for Sunday supper.

DRESSING

75 ml  *3 fluid oz white wine
vinegar*
225 ml  *8 fluid oz oil (olive,
if possible)
½ teaspoon sugar
Salt and pepper
1 clove of garlic*

Mix all the salad dressing ingredients in a measuring jug.

Keep in container in fridge and use 4 to 6 tablespoons for this salad.

## ORANGE MERINGUE PUDDING

This pudding is like soft ice-cream and meringue. It has to be made a day in advance.

MERINGUE

*3 egg whites*
150 g  *6 oz castor sugar
Pinch of salt*

Add salt to egg whites and beat until stiff. Add sugar slowly, beating well between each addition. Pipe or spoon on to lightly oiled baking tray and place in cool oven, 200°F 100°C gas ¼, for 3–4 hours. Store in airtight container when dried out.

ORANGE CREAM

150 ml  *½ pint double cream
Grated rind and juice
of 1 orange
1 tablespoon orange
curaçao or brandy*

Whip cream until stiff and slowly beat in rind and juice with brandy. Be careful not to add too much liquid or the mixture will curdle.

Break half of meringue into pieces and fold into cream mixture. Put into 1½-pint (750-ml) mixing bowl and place in freezer. One hour before serving dip bowl into hot water and turn out on to serving dish, but leave with bowl on top until ready to serve. If kitchen is warm, place in fridge. At the last minute decorate with rest of meringues, grated orange rind or orange slices.

---

# Saturday Dinner

## (for 8 people)

### COD WITH PRAWNS AND OLIVES

| | |
|---|---|
| 750 g | 1½ lb cod fillet |
| 250 g | 8 oz prawns |
| | 10–12 black olives |
| | 5–6 peppercorns |
| | Salt |
| | 2 bay leaves |
| | 2 tablespoons chopped shallots or onion |
| | Whole prawns to decorate |
| | 2 tablespoons chopped parsley |

Place cod in ovenproof dish, cover with water, add salt, peppercorns and bay leaves. Poach in oven, 350°F 180°C gas 4, for 20 minutes. Break up fish into 1-inch (2-cm) pieces and when cool add prawns, onion, parsley and olives. Season well.

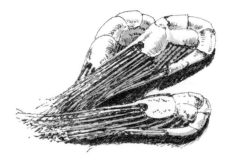

**LIME VINAIGRETTE**

2 tablespoons lime juice
5 tablespoons olive oil
Salt and pepper
½ clove garlic chopped (optional)

Lime juice is available in plastic squeeze bottles. Fresh limes are of course better if you can get them.

Mix well together, pour over fish and mix carefully. Place in mould on serving dish, decorate with prawns or lime and lemon slices. Serve with Aïoli sauce.

**AIOLI SAUCE**

| | |
|---|---|
| | 1 egg yolk |
| 150 ml | ¼ pint oil |
| | Squeeze of lemon juice |
| | Salt and pepper |
| | 1 clove garlic |
| | 1 tablespoon cream |

Make ¼ pint (150 ml) of mayonnaise. (Beat egg yolk in small bowl, add a drop of oil and beat. Continue adding oil very slowly, beating all the time. Add lemon juice and season.) Crush garlic and mix to a cream with salt, add to mayonnaise and lastly add cream.

This can be made in advance and stored in fridge.

### LOIN OF PORK WITH WINE AND HERBS

2–2½ kg    *1 rolled loin of pork,*
*approximately 4–5 lb*
*with skin removed. Keep*
*the bones to make a stock*
*3 tablespoons lard or*
*pork fat*
*1 sliced onion*
*1 sliced carrot*
*1 bouquet garni (4 parsley*
*sprigs, ½ bay leaf*
*¼ teaspoon thyme)*

MARINADE, per pound
(500 g) of pork
*1 teaspoon salt*
*⅛ teaspoon ground pepper*
*¼ teaspoon thyme or sage*
*⅛ teaspoon ground bayleaf*
*Pinch of allspice*
*½ clove garlic (optional)*

GRAVY
150 ml    *¼ pint white wine*
150 ml    *¼ pint pork stock*

GLAZED CARROTS
1 kg    *2 lb carrots, sliced*
*lengthwise*
425 ml    *¾ pint stock (or water)*
*2 tablespoons granulated*
*sugar*
75 g    *3 oz butter*
*Salt and pepper*

Make the marinade on Friday.

Mix all the marinade ingredients together and rub them into the surface of the meat. Place in a covered bowl and leave for 24 hours, turning the meat two or three times. Before cooking scrape off marinade and dry meat thoroughly.

Heat the lard or pork fat in an ovenproof casserole until almost smoking. Brown meat on all sides, which will take about 8–10 minutes. Remove and drain fat, leaving 1 tablespoon. Add the onion, carrot and bouquet garni.

Cover casserole and cook for 5 minutes, then return meat to casserole. Cover and place in oven, 325°F 170°C gas 3, for 2 hours. Baste 2 or 3 times. When cooked remove pork, discard trussing strings, carefully carve and arrange on serving dish and keep warm.

Pour the wine and stock into casserole and simmer slowly for 5 minutes. Tilt casserole and skim off fat. Mash vegetables into the juices and boil again for a few minutes. Strain and pour some over meat and put the remainder into a gravy boat.

Serve with glazed carrots, purée of spinach and baked apples.

Boil carrots in covered saucepan with all ingredients until liquid has reduced to a syrupy glaze, about 30–40 minutes. Turn into serving dish and sprinkle with chopped parsley

# Saturday Dinner

continued

---

**PUREE OF SPINACH**

1¼ kg   *3 lb fresh spinach*
*Salt and pepper*
*3 tablespoons cream or milk*
25 g   *1 oz butter*

Remove stalks and wash well. Place in a covered saucepan with butter, salt and pepper and cook until soft. Purée in blender, adding cream and mixing well.

**BAKED APPLES**

*4 even-sized cooking apples*
*Watercress*

Core apples and cut in half horizontally. Place cut side up in baking dish with ½ inch of water. Sprinkle lightly with sugar and bake for 20–30 minutes depending on size of apples. Place around meat and at the last minute stuff with watercress leaves just before serving.

I would prepare all these vegetables on Saturday afternoon.

## CHOCOLATE ROULADE

This must be made at least a day in advance.

    *5 eggs*
175 g   *6 oz castor sugar*
175 g   *6 oz bitter chocolate*
    *2 tablespoons water*

**FILLING**

150 ml   *¼ pint whipped cream*
*1 tablespoon brandy or*
*1 teaspoon vanilla*

**DECORATION**

*Icing sugar*
*Toasted almonds*

Prepare a Swiss roll tin by lining with greased greaseproof paper, slit paper at corners and fold to make box. Secure with butcher's pins or large paper clips – never pins as one may be lost during cooking.

    Melt chocolate with water in bowl over hot water. Separate eggs, add sugar to yolks and beat until white and fluffy. Add melted chocolate. Whisk egg whites until stiff and fold into mixture. Pour into prepared tin. Drop the tin on the worktop from a height of about 1 inch (3 cm) to let out large air bubbles and bake at 375°F 190°C gas 5 for 18 minutes.

When cooked cool and leave in tin covered with a damp tea towel until next day. Spread with whipped cream flavoured with brandy and carefully roll, removing greaseproof paper. Wrap paper round roll and place in fridge. Just before serving sprinkle with sieved icing sugar and almonds.

---

# Sunday Lunch

(for 6 people)

## LEG OF LAMB IN LEMON AND GARLIC CRUST

LEMON AND
GARLIC CRUST

270 g  *10 oz plain flour*
     *1 level teaspoon salt*
     *2 tablespoons lemon juice*
     *2 tablespoons cold water*
     *1–2 cloves of garlic*
150 g  *5 oz butter*
     *1 egg*

Either buy a 5-lb ($2\frac{1}{4}$-kg) leg of lamb on the bone or have the butcher remove the bone, which makes carving easier. You will have to discard trussing string as it is carved or use butcher's skewers pierced through the base of the crust if the joint has been boned. Slip slivers of garlic deep into the cuts in the meat if you wish.

Cream garlic into salt. Sift flour on to large board or clean worktop. Make well in centre and add salt and garlic and lemon juice and water. Cut butter into pieces and add this with the egg. Mix with fingers, gradually drawing in flour. Knead until smooth and chill 1–2 hours or until required.*

Roll out pastry $\frac{1}{8}$–$\frac{1}{4}$ inch (3–5 mm) thick. Wrap around meat, sealing well, and use trimmings for decoration. Brush with beaten egg and cook in oven, 375°F 190°C gas 5, for $1\frac{1}{2}$ hours. If pastry is getting too brown cover with foil. Test if meat is cooked by piercing with a skewer and leaving in for 1 minute. Pull out and feel the end. If it is cold the meat is not cooked enough; if warm the meat is pink inside; if hot the meat is well done.

Serve with gravy or Batarde sauce.

*Pastry can be made in advance and stored in fridge.

BATARDE SAUCE

 20 g  *$\frac{3}{4}$ oz butter*
 20 g  *$\frac{3}{4}$ oz flour*
275 ml  *$\frac{1}{2}$ pint hot water*
     *2 egg yolks*
     *Salt and pepper*
     *A few drops of lemon juice*
 50 g  *2 oz butter*
     *1–2 tablespoons green*
       *peppercorns*

Melt butter in saucepan, stir in flour off heat. Beat water slowly into yolks and add all at once to roux. Whisk briskly until just on boiling point, add butter in small pieces. Add lemon juice and drained peppercorns. Do not boil.

Serve with roast potatoes (see page 31), 1 lb (500 g) petit pois (frozen packet), and 1 large cauliflower (divided into florets, stirred in frying pan for 1 minute with 1 oz (25 g) butter, $\frac{1}{4}$ teaspoon crushed coriander seeds, 1 tablespoon parsley, salt and pepper, then covered and cooked for 4 minutes more).

# Sunday Lunch

continued

## RHUBARB CRUMBLE

1 kg    *2 lb rhubarb stalks*
      *2–3 cups granulated sugar*
150 ml  *¼ pint orange juice*

**CRUMBLE**

175 g   *6 oz plain flour*
75 g    *3 oz butter*
175 g   *6 oz brown or white sugar*

Make the crumble: mix together the flour and the butter as for pastry until it resembles breadcrumbs. Stir in the sugar. (Or put it all in the Magimix).*

Cut the rhubarb into 3-inch (7-cm) lengths, place in a saucepan and stir in the sugar and orange juice. Cook very gently for 5–10 minutes until the rhubarb is becoming soft, but not mushy. Turn into an ovenproof dish and spoon out any excess moisture if it is very liquid, otherwise it will boil over the crumble. Spread the crumble on the top of the rhubarb and cook in oven, 375°F 190°C gas 5, for 20 minutes.

*The crumble can be prepared a day or so in advance and kept in the fridge. It also freezes.

# Sunday Supper

(for 2 people)

## SALAD SOUP

*1 can tomato juice*
*Dash of Worcester sauce*
   *and Tabasco*
*Salt and pepper*

A ½-pint (150-ml) mixing bowl filled with left-over salad (dressed). If not enough add more lettuce, cucumber, tomato etc.

Place all the ingredients in a liquidizer and blend until the desired consistency is reached. I prefer it not too smooth. Chill.

PREPARATION TIME 5 minutes.

## POTTED SHRIMPS AND SCRAMBLED EGGS

*2 small cartons potted*
   *shrimps*
*4–6 eggs*
*2 tablespoons cream*
*Salt and pepper*
*1 tablespoon parsley,*
   *chopped*

Defrost the potted shrimps and place in a saucepan. Heat very gently until the butter has melted. Lightly beat the eggs, cream, parsley, salt and pepper and add to the shrimps. Cook, stirring continuously, until the mixture becomes creamy scrambled eggs. Pile on to buttered toast and serve immediately, perhaps with a green salad.

Follow with cheese.

*The Cottage was originally built*
*as two cottages – each one-up and one-down*
*– at the turn of the nineteenth*
*century. It is believed to have been the toll*
*keeper's house when the old Salisbury road*
*crossed the river nearby. The bridge*
*has since been moved and the road is now a*
*footpath. The Cottage's original thatch*
*has been replaced by slate.*

# MAY

# Toby Eady

 The refreshing thing about Toby is that he is unable to make a white sauce. This would hinder most people from attempting a dinner party, let alone a weekend. He is also hampered by a kitchen of great antiquity: he has no deep freeze, no electric blender or mixer, and works on an electric cooker with only two rings. He has no working surface save the top of the fridge or the draining board. He also has to contend with a constant flow of traffic, since his kitchen is the approach to the stairs. Finally, he has often flown from New York the previous day. And yet he always produces the most delicious food.

'I cook quickly, as being a bachelor I have no time to prepare anything. I love very simple food. Most of my recipes I have adapted myself. I lie in bed in the morning thinking about tastes. Although I have never learnt to cook, and as most people only learn to cook when they marry, I never rely on help from a girl friend. Having lived in India I use spices a lot and always have a stock of strong-tasting things like capers, anchovies, olives and juniper berries, lots of herbs and crushed red peppers.'

He is unable to keep stocks of anything perishable as he is often away from the cottage for weeks; he also has to adapt his cooking to his facilities – which is why, with only two rings, many of his vegetables are roasted.

'I always cook pasta on Friday night – it is ideal to give people who have just driven down from London. Pasta is an excellent blotting paper to soak up a heavy week. I think it very important to have fresh pasta, which I buy in Soho. It is damp, all pasta should be damp; it is also much quicker to cook.

'I don't like sauces. I can't be bothered to garnish my food, but colour is important. My recipes rarely take much time to prepare, with the exception of the goose; that is delicious, very rich, and should be eaten with its salad stuffing and roast turnips.

## Friday

Green and White Pasta with Cream, Mushrooms, Peas and Ham
Green Salad

Dolcelatte and Italian Bread

## Saturday

LUNCH

Cod Brazilian Style
Boiled Potatoes
Green Salad with Fresh Mint

Strawberries and Thick Cream

DINNER

Shrimps and Broad Beans with Cumin

Baby Legs of Lamb
New Potatoes roasted in Sage and Rosemary
Carrots

Gaperon Cheese with Bath Oliver Biscuits
Fresh Fruit

## Sunday

LUNCH

Roast Guinea Fowl
Peas
Rice

Columbert Cheese
Green Salad

Preserved Stem Ginger and Cream

SUPPER

Cold Lamb
Green Salad

# MAY

# Friday Supper

(for 6 people)

### GREEN AND WHITE PASTA WITH CREAM, MUSHROOMS, PEAS AND HAM

| | |
|---|---|
| 350 g | *12 oz mushrooms, sliced* |
| | *Oil and butter* |
| 50 g | *2 oz Spek, chopped fine* |
| 100 g | *4 oz peas* |
| 150 ml | *¼ pint single cream* |
| 350 g | *12 oz green pasta* |
| 350 g | *12 oz white pasta* |
| 100 g | *4 oz freshly grated* |
| | *Parmesan* |

The pasta I use for this is very thin: it is called 'hay and straw'. It should be bought fresh (I get mine from Old Compton Street, Soho) and can be deep frozen. Spek is a north Italian smoked ham, available in most good supermarkets. Smoked bacon would do as an alternative.

Put the mushrooms and Spek in a small pan with enough oil to cover the bottom of the pan and a nut of butter. Cook very slowly over a gentle heat for 15 minutes. Add the peas and cook for a further 3 minutes. Remove from the heat.

Fill a large pot with boiling water, plenty of salt and a drop of oil and cook the white pasta only for 4 minutes. Add the green pasta and let them swim together for a further 4 minutes. Warm a large bowl and pour in the cream, then the sauce. Drain the pasta and mix in with the sauce and cream. Have a bowlful of freshly grated Parmesan and a black pepper mill on the table and serve immediately.

PREPARATION AND COOKING TIME 30 minutes.

Afterwards have a large green salad made from Cos Lettuce and serve it with a large slice of Dolcelatte cheese and Italian bread, which you can buy when getting the fresh pasta.

# Saturday Lunch

## (for 6 people)

### COD BRAZILIAN STYLE

750 g   *1½ lb cod fillets*
2 × 400 g   *2 × 14 oz cans of tomatoes*
    *(or 1 lb–500 g–of fresh ones)*
*Approximately 16 small*
    *black olives, with stones*
*1 small clove garlic, crushed*
*Ground black pepper*
*Salt*

Drain the tomatoes or roughly chop the fresh ones. (I never skin mine.) Put the tomatoes, olives, garlic, pepper and salt in a pan and cook slowly for about 15 minutes (less if you are using tinned tomatoes).

Put the fish into an ovenproof dish, pour on the sauce and cook in the oven at 375–400°F 190–200°C gas 5–6 for 10 minutes. Take out and sprinkle with parsley.

Serve with one small boiled potato per person and a green salad, with a light vinaigrette which has 1 tablespoon of fresh chopped mint added.

Strawberries and thick cream to follow.

# Saturday Dinner

## (for 8 people)

### SHRIMPS AND BROAD BEANS WITH CUMIN

225 g   *8 oz peeled frozen shrimps*
450 g   *1 lb frozen broad beans*
    *2 teaspoons cumin*
    *(according to taste)*
    *Butter*

Sauté the shrimps in butter and cumin very slowly for 15 minutes. Add the broad beans and stir or shake the pan for 4–5 minutes. Have guests sitting and serve immediately.

### BABY LEGS OF LAMB (for Mr Pollock)

2 × 1–1½ kg   *2 small legs of lamb,*
    *2½–3 lb each*
    *Butter*
    *Salt and pepper*

Salt, pepper and butter the joints. Cook one leg for those who like well-done meat, and one for those who like it rare. I just cook one leg about 30 minutes longer, but the leg I eat for never more than 13 minutes to the lb in a hot oven, 450°F 230°C gas 8.

Take the legs out together and let them sit while eating the previous course.

Serve with new potatoes roasted in oil with a knob of butter for 45 minutes; and steamed baby carrots cooked in ½ inch (1 cm) water.

Then a Gaperon cheese with Bath Oliver biscuits, and fresh fruit.

# Sunday Lunch

(for 6 people)

### ROAST GUINEA FOWL

1 – 1½ kg   *3 small guinea fowl or*
*2 large ones*
*Few sprigs of rosemary*
*Oil and butter*

Stuff the birds with sprigs of rosemary and roast for 1 hour in butter and oil in a hot oven, 425°F 220°C gas 7, for the first 10 minutes, slowing down and then ending high for the last 10 minutes. Serve with frozen petit pois and rice.

I would follow this with a whole Columbert cheese (which can be got from any delicatessen) and a green salad. And finally preserved ginger (which you can buy in jars from a delicatessen) with cream.

# Sunday Supper

(for 2 people)

Cold lamb with salad

# Sally Worthington

**Friday**

SUPPER

Egg and Tomato Mousse with Garlic Bread

Noisettes of Lamb in White Wine
Julienne of Spring Vegetables

**Saturday**

LUNCH

Pork and Apple Pie
Broad Bean and Gruyère Cheese Salad

Meringues filled with Whipped Cream and Chocolate

DINNER

Green Pepper Soup

Cold Salmon Trout and Watercress Mousseline
New Potatoes
Salad

Hot Asparagus and Melted Butter

**Sunday**

LUNCH

Duck in Orange Jelly
Orange and Pasta Salad
Green Salad

Rhubarb Streusal Pie

SUPPER

Spring Vegetable Soup

Home-made Sausages
Hot Potato Salad

# Friday Supper
## (for 6 people)

### EGG AND TOMATO MOUSSE

| | |
|---|---|
| 125 ml | *5 fluid oz tomato cocktail* |
| 2 × 400 g | *2 × 14 oz tins tomatoes* |
| 350 g | *12 oz fresh tomatoes,* |
| | *skinned* |
| 275 ml | *½ pint sour cream* |
| | *10 hard-boiled eggs* |
| | *2 tablespoons herbs* |
| | *(parsley, thyme etc.)* |
| | *2 tablespoons lemon juice* |
| | *1 tablespoon tomato purée* |
| 25 g | *1 oz gelatine* |
| | *½ teaspoon sugar* |
| | *A dash of Worcester sauce* |

Put the canned tomatoes in a sieve to drain. Put fresh and canned tomatoes through a Mouli (or liquidize then sieve), season well with salt and pepper, sugar, tomato purée and Worcester sauce. Soften the gelatine in the lemon juice and add to the tomato cocktail. Heat gently until dissolved. Cool, then blend in tomato mixture. Add chopped hard-boiled eggs, herbs and sour cream. Put into soufflé dish and leave in fridge until set.

This can be made on Thursday.

PREPARATION TIME 30 minutes.

#### FRESH TOMATO SAUCE

| | |
|---|---|
| 450 g | *1 lb tomatoes, skinned* |
| | *and deseeded* |
| | *1 tablespoon olive oil* |
| | *1 teaspoon castor sugar* |
| | *1 tablespoon basil or mint* |
| | *Salt and freshly ground* |
| | *pepper* |

Purée all this together and season to taste. Serve with the tomato mousse.

### NOISETTES OF LAMB IN WHITE WINE

| | |
|---|---|
| | *12 lamb cutlets made into* |
| | *noisettes* |
| | *12–16 button onions* |
| 350 g | *12 oz sliced mushrooms* |
| | *16–18 small new potatoes* |
| 450 g | *1 lb frozen peas* |
| 275 ml | *½ pint white wine* |
| | *1 tablespoon butter* |
| | *1 tablespoon oil* |
| | *Sprig of rosemary* |
| | *Parsley* |
| | *Salt and pepper* |

Flour the noisettes and fry gently in the oil and butter to brown. Put into a casserole. Fry the button onions until brown (if you are unable to get them use spring onions). Add to lamb. Season with salt and pepper and a good pinch of rosemary. Pour off excess fat from the frying pan and add white wine, bring to the boil and pour over the chops and onions. Add the small new potatoes, cover and cook for ¾ hour at 350°F 180°C gas 4. Add the sliced mushrooms and peas and cook for a further ¼ hour. Serve with a good garnish of chopped parsley.

PREPARATION TIME 20 minutes    COOKING TIME 1 hour.

# Friday Supper

### continued

JULIENNE OF
SPRING VEGETABLES

4 *large or 6 small carrots*
4 *sticks celery*
*A little fennel*
1 *large onion or 2 leeks*
150 ml  ¼ *pint chicken stock*
2 *level teaspoons butter*
2 *level teaspoons flour*
*Parsley*

This can also be made with any other root vegetables in season, such as turnips, parsnips or swedes.

Cut the vegetables into even-sized julienne strips, about ⅛ inch (3 mm) wide and 2 inches (50 mm) long. Blanch in boiling water for 5 minutes. Put into heat-proof dish and season well. Add chicken stock, cover and cook in oven until tender – about 30 minutes.

Before serving stir in *beurre manié* of butter worked with the flour until blended. Sprinkle with parsley.

MAY

# Saturday Lunch

(for 6 people)

## PORK AND APPLE PIE

| | |
|---|---|
| 225 g | *Shortcrust pastry made with 8 oz flour (see page 127)* |
| 750 g | *1½ lb minced pork* |
| 125 g | *4 oz bacon, rinded and chopped* |
| | *1 large onion, chopped* |
| | *2 sharp apples, cored, peeled and chopped* |
| | *1–2 tablespoons cider* |
| | *Egg to glaze* |
| | *Salt and pepper* |
| | *Sea salt crystals* |
| | *Rosemary* |
| | *Nutmeg* |
| | *Allspice* |

I think that cheese goes very well with pork and apples. I sometimes make this pie with cheese pastry; and I serve it with a cheese and bean salad.

Divide the pastry into two and use half to line an 8-inch (20-cm) sandwich tin or pie plate. Put the minced pork into a basin and add chopped onion, bacon and apple. Season with rosemary, salt, pepper and nutmeg (or mace). Add the cider and mix well together. Spoon into case and cover with the rest of pastry which has been rolled out into a round.

Seal the edges, decorate and glaze with an egg beaten with a pinch of salt. Sprinkle top with sea salt crystals, ground pepper, nutmeg and allspice. Bake near the top of the oven for 20 minutes at 400°F 200°C gas 6. Reduce heat to 375°F 190°C gas 5 for a further 45 minutes.

## BROAD BEAN AND GRUYÈRE CHEESE SALAD

| | |
|---|---|
| 450 g | *1 lb broad beans* |
| 125 g | *4 oz mushrooms* |
| | *1 shallot or 2 spring onions, finely chopped* |
| 175 g | *6 oz Gruyère or other cheese* |
| | *Olive oil* |
| | *2 tablespoons French dressing* |
| | *Watercress or lettuce* |

You can also make this with little cubes of Cheshire or Caerphilly.

Sauté the mushrooms (sliced if large) quickly in olive oil. Set aside and while still warm moisten with 1–2 tablespoons of vinaigrette. Barely cook the beans, so that they are still firm. Cut the cheese into little cubes and mix everything together. Season well, adding a little more vinaigrette if necessary. Serve in lettuce- or watercress-lined bowl.

## MERINGUES FILLED WITH WHIPPED CREAM AND CHOCOLATE

| | |
|---|---|
| | *6 egg whites* |
| 350 g | *12 oz castor sugar* |
| | *2 tablespoons good plain chocolate, grated* |
| 275 ml | *½ pint double cream, whipped* |

To make the meringues: whip the whites very, very stiff. Add 1 tablespoon of castor sugar, mix well, then add half the rest of the sugar, mix well again and add the other half. Spoon on to a greased baking sheet and bake in a very low oven, 200°F 100°C gas low, for about 3 hours or until set.*

Whip the cream and stir in the grated chocolate, fill the meringues and dust with chocolate powder.

*Can be made well in advance and stored in a tin.

# Saturday Dinner

## (for 8 people)

### GREEN PEPPER SOUP

| | |
|---|---|
| | 2 tablespoons oil |
| 50 g | 2 oz butter |
| 275 g | 10 oz green peppers, seeded and diced |
| | 2 medium onions, chopped |
| 30 g | 1½ oz flour |
| 575 ml | 1 pint chicken stock |
| 575 ml | 1 pint milk |
| 275 ml | ½ pint single cream |
| | Salt and pepper |

Setting aside some of the chopped pepper for a garnish, cook the rest with the onions gently in oil and butter until slightly softened (about 5 minutes). Blend in the flour and cook for one minute. Stir in stock gradually and bring to the boil. Season well and cover and simmer for 30 minutes. Put through Mouli or liquidize, then sieve. Add the milk and heat through.* Stir in the cream just before serving. Top with finely chopped peppers, parsley or a slice of lemon.

This is also delicious cold, in which case swirl the cream through at the last moment after chilling.

*This can be prepared in advance.

### SALMON TROUT

| | |
|---|---|
| 3 kg | 1 large salmon trout, about 6 lb |
| | Butter |
| | Parsley, dill or any other herb |
| | Salt and pepper |

Butter a sheet of foil liberally, put the chopped herbs and seasoning in the fish and wrap in tin foil. Put a little water into a roasting dish and put in trout. Cook in a medium oven, 350°F 180°C gas 5, for 1 hour.

#### WATERCRESS MOUSSELINE

| | |
|---|---|
| | 2 bunches of watercress |
| 275 ml | ½ pint double cream |
| | Juice of half a lemon |
| | Salt and freshly ground pepper |

Discard most of the thick stems of watercress and blanch it in boiling water until soft (5–10 minutes). Sieve or purée. Bring the cream to the boil. Add the watercress and season well. Chill. Just before serving whisk, adding the lemon juice gradually until thick.

### HOT ASPARAGUS AND BUTTER

| | |
|---|---|
| ½ kg | 8–10 stems of asparagus per person |
| ½ kg | 1 lb butter, melted |

Cut the stalks the same size and lightly scrape the white part of each with a sharp knife. Arrange in bunches not bigger than your hand can hold and tied in the middle, plunge into boiling salted water, heads uppermost and out of the water. Cook until just tender. This varies according to age and size but it should be 12–14 minutes after the water has returned to boiling point. Freshly cut garden asparagus may take less time. Serve with hot butter in a separate dish.

# Sunday Lunch

(for 6 people)

### DUCK IN ORANGE JELLY

This should be made a day in advance.

| | |
|---|---|
| 2½ kg | *1 large Aylesbury duck, 5–6 lb, jointed into small portions* |
| | *Butter and oil* |
| 150 ml | *¼ pint white wine* |
| 575 ml | *1 pint stock* |
| | *Bouquet garni* |
| 50 g | *2 oz streaky bacon, cubed* |
| | *8–10 button mushrooms* |
| | *8–10 button onions* |
| | *Grated peel and juice of 1 orange and ½ lemon* |
| | *2 level tablespoons gelatine* |
| | *2 egg whites and shells* |
| | *Salt and freshly ground black pepper* |

Sauté the duck in a casserole in a mixture of oil and butter until golden. Add the wine and stock and bring to the boil. Add the seasoning and bouquet garni. In a fry pan sauté the bacon and onions until golden. Sauté the mushrooms and add them together with the bacon and onions to the casserole. Cover and simmer for 1½ hours or until tender, basting from time to time.

Put the duck pieces into a flattish round or oval dish that is just big enough to hold them, surround with the bacon, mushrooms and onions. Strain the stock into a bowl. Cool and remove fat from the surface. Clarify the stock by whipping the egg whites until they are just frothy and then adding them to the stock with the egg shells. Bring to the boil, whisking all the time. As soon as it boils, stop whisking and allow the mixture to come to the top of the pan; remove from the heat and leave for 10 minutes. Strain through a cold wet cloth. Add the fruit juice and peel. Soften the gelatine in a little cold water and add to the hot stock. Spoon over the duck to cover and chill overnight.

PREPARATION TIME 45 minutes   COOKING TIME 1½ hours.

### ORANGE AND PASTA SALAD

| | |
|---|---|
| 225 g | *8 oz pasta shells or other shapes* |
| | *2 oranges, peeled and divided into segments* |
| | *4 chopped spring onions* |
| 150 ml | *¼ pint sour cream* |
| | *4 tablespoons orange juice* |
| | *2 tablespoons olive oil* |
| | *1 tablespoon chopped mint* |

Cook the pasta shells *al dente* (still firm). Drain and rinse in cold water. Season well. Mix in orange segments and spring onions. Mix the sour cream, orange juice, oil and mint together and pour over the pasta. Cover with cling film and leave till needed.

I would also serve a plain green salad with this.

### RHUBARB STREUSAL PIE

PASTRY

225 g  *8 oz plain flour*
125 g  *4 oz butter*
      *2 tablespoons castor sugar*
      *3 tablespoons cold milk*

FILLING

450 g  *1 lb rhubarb*

STREUSAL

125 g  *4 oz self-raising flour*
75 g  *3 oz butter*
50 g  *2 oz castor sugar*

First make the pastry. Sift the flour into a bowl and rub in the butter. Add the sugar and milk and mix together with a fork. Turn out and knead slightly to make a dough.* Roll out and line an 8-inch (20-cm) flan dish. Bake blind until set but not brown (about 10 minutes in a hot oven).

Chop the rhubarb into 1-inch (2-cm) pieces. Make the streusal by rubbing the flour, butter and sugar together until they look like breadcrumbs. Sprinkle a little over the base of the flan, add the rhubarb and top with the rest of the streusal mixture. Bake at 375°F 190°C gas 5 for 35 minutes.

PREPARATION TIME 15 minutes    COOKING TIME 35 minutes.

*The pastry can be mixed in advance and kept in the refrigerator.

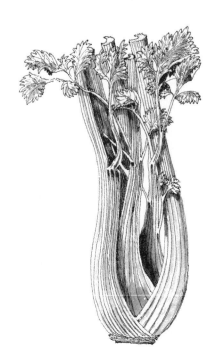

# Sunday Supper

(for 2 people)

---

425 ml · ¾ *pint chicken stock*
*Bouquet garni: a bay leaf and parsley*
*2 carrots*
*½ onion*
*1 stalk celery*
*Parsnip*
*Potato*
*A few frozen peas*
*A few basil leaves*
*½ clove garlic*

To make 1 lb (500 g) sausages:

500 g · *1 lb belly pork, minced, using a good proportion of fat to keep the sausages tender*
*1 medium onion*
*Thyme or any herb you like*
*1 tablespoon parsley*
*Salt and freshly ground black pepper*
*Sausage casings*
*1 bay leaf*
*Mace and nutmeg*
*1 clove garlic*

HOT POTATO SALAD
(for 2 people)

*2 rashers of bacon, rinded*
*3 medium potatoes*
*3 tablespoons olive oil*
*1 dessertspoon white wine vinegar*
*1 teaspoon French mustard*
*Salt and freshly ground black pepper*
*Finely chopped chives for garnishing*

## SPRING VEGETABLE SOUP

This can be made with any mixture of root vegetables.

Dice all the vegetables, put into saucepan and add the stock, bouquet garni, salt and pepper. Simmer until soft (about 30 minutes). Pound the basil leaves and garlic together and add to the soup with a few frozen peas. Stir well and serve.

This freezes well without the basil and garlic.

## HOME-MADE SAUSAGES

These can be made either in a mixer or in a forcing bag with a wide nozzle. They are delicious fresh, but they freeze very well. Sausage casings are available from most butchers; they come with instructions.

Crush the bay leaf and chop the onion finely. Mix with all the other ingredients by hand. (Omit the garlic if you do not like it.) Soak the casings first and attach them to the mincer (using someone to help if possible). Fill the casings and tie or twist to make sausages.

Boil the potatoes until just cooked and still firm. Fry diced bacon until the fat runs and the bacon is crisp. Make a vinaigrette with the oil and vinegar, add the mustard and seasonings and mix well. Pour over the potatoes while still warm. Add the bacon, toss and sprinkle with chives.

---

The village in which Godsfield Manor lies was described by John Duthy in *Sketches of Hampshire* (1839) as an 'unnoticed extra-parochial hamlet . . . that is worth observation'. Next to the main house is a thirteenth-century chapel made from limestone and flint, which on special occasions is Kate's dining room. (It is deconsecrated.) Her kitchen smells of France, with bundles of rosemary hanging from the ceiling and a large, freshly picked bunch of herbs on the kitchen table. 'They are pretty,' says Kate, 'and I can use them for cooking.' Flowers play a big part in Kate's life: the house is always brimming over with them, and the smell in June of the musk and damask roses is exquisite.

'Flowers, fires, music and good smells are all very important for me. Everything has to be relaxed to make a happy atmosphere. I have to plan ahead as I'm in London in the middle of the week, and I must have time during the weekend to be with my friends, go riding or whatever, and not always be in the kitchen. I shop twice weekly, and plan meals around the vegetable garden, arriving in London on Tuesday laden with fruit, flowers and vegetables and returning on Friday morning or Thursday evening.

'Weather permitting breakfast in the country is outside, otherwise it's in the kitchen. There are always bowls of fresh fruit, home-made brown bread, home-made crab apple and geranium jelly, honey, and free-range eggs which are either scrambled, boiled or fried with bacon and fried bread. And plenty of good coffee.

'When I was first married saucepans were known to go flying in my husband's direction! But I love having the house full of friends, and luckily with practice I've learnt to be organized, which makes everything so much more fun.'

*The chapel at Godsfield was built*
*by the Knights of St John of Jerusalem in the*
*early thirteenth century.*

# JUNE

## Kate Vey

## Friday

**SUPPER**

Zadziki

Pork Fillet with Hot Fruit Salad
Baked Potatoes
Avocado Pear and Watercress Salad

Brie and Black Grapes

## Saturday

**LUNCH**

Quiche aux Herbes
Mixed Salad

Rhubarb and Ginger Ice Cream
Tuiles d'Amandes or Belgian Chocolate Biscuits

**DINNER**

Scallop and Prawn Pancake with Tomato and Garlic Sauce

Roast Rolled Sirloin of Beef
Green Hollandaise Sauce
Fennel
Broccoli
Roast Potatoes

Peppermint Roulade

## Sunday

**LUNCH**

Chilled Carrot and Orange Soup

Stuffed Leg of Veal
Sauté Potatoes
Mange Tout
Purée of Spinach

Gooseberry Fool and Fork Biscuits

**SUPPER**

Broccoli and Fennel Soup

Scrambled Eggs with Bacon and Croûtons
Cheese and Fruit

# Friday Supper

## (for 6 people)

---

### ZADZIKI

| | |
|---|---|
| | *2 large cucumbers* |
| 700 ml | *24 fluid oz (1½ large cartons) natural yogurt* |
| | *3 tablespoons best olive oil (green if possible)* |
| | *4 cloves of garlic, crushed* |
| | *Salt and pepper* |
| | *1 large tablespoon chopped parsley* |

This is a delicious Greek recipe and is very quick and simple to make.

Peel and grate the cucumbers. Cover with salt and leave for 1 hour. Rinse well with plenty of cold water and squeeze dry in a tea towel. Mix the cucumber with the yogurt and garlic and stir in the olive oil. Season to taste. Decorate with chopped parsley and serve with hot brown toast.

### PORK FILLET WITH HOT FRUIT SALAD

| | |
|---|---|
| | *6 slices pork fillet banged out thin* |
| 225 g each | *1 small can each of* |
| | *Peach halves* |
| | *Pineapple chunks* |
| | *Mandarin oranges* |
| | *Apricots* |
| | *Purple plums* |
| 450 g | *1 lb fresh cherries, stoned* |
| | *Purple sage and borage or other fresh herbs* |
| | *Seasoning* |
| | *Origano* |
| | **SAUCE** |
| 50 g | *2 oz butter* |
| | *2 level teaspoons plain flour* |
| | *1 tablespoon sugar* |
| | *1 teaspoon salt* |
| 150 ml | *1 cup of reserved fruit juice* |
| | *1½ teaspoons curry powder* |
| | *Juice of ½ lemon* |
| 120 ml | *¾ cup of sherry or dry martini* |

To make the sauce, drain the tinned fruit, reserving 1 cup of the juice. Melt the butter in a saucepan and stir in the flour; when the roux is smooth add the sugar, salt and fruit juice and stir until smooth and thick. Then add the curry powder, lemon juice and alcohol, and pour over the strained fruit.* Bake for 1 hour in a slow oven, 300–350°F 150–180°C gas 2–4. Add the fresh cherries just before serving.

Season the fillets with salt, pepper and origano and fry in olive oil and butter over a gentle heat until golden and cooked through, about 6 minutes. Keep warm.

Bake 6 potatoes for 1 hour in a hot oven, 400°F 200°C gas 6.

To serve, heap baked potatoes, split open and stuffed with butter, on a large dish and arrange pork fillets around them. Decorate with purple sage and borage. Serve the sauce separately. A good wine to accompany this would be Antinori Classico Chianti.

*This much can be done the day before.

---

AVOCADO PEAR AND
WATERCRESS SALAD

*2 avocado pears*
*4 bunches watercress*
*Walnuts to garnish*

FRENCH DRESSING

*2 tablespoons best olive oil*
*4 tablespoons vegetable oil*
*3 tablespoons wine vinegar*
*1 whole egg*
*Salt and pepper*
*1 tablespoon French mustard*
*1 dessertspoon sugar*
*Squeeze of lemon juice*

Beat everything together until thick (I use a Magimix)
   To serve, arrange the avocado and watercress in a large bowl and sprinkle with walnuts. Serve the French dressing separately.

## BRIE AND BLACK GRAPES

Serve the whole bunch of grapes on the cheese board with the Brie and hot wholemeal bread.

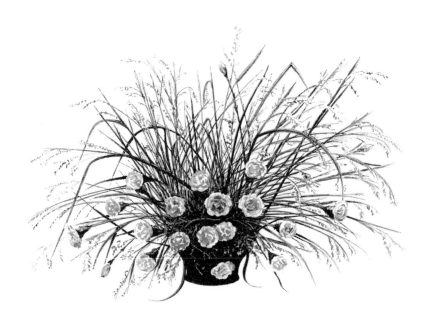

# Saturday Lunch in the garden

## (for 6 people)

---

### QUICHE AUX HERBES

#### PASTRY

250 g   *9 oz plain flour*
175 g   *6 oz butter*
         *1 egg yolk*
         *3 tablespoons cold water*

#### FILLING

         *5 whole eggs*
         *5 egg yolks*
575 ml   *1 pint milk or single cream*
         *1 large handful grated*
           *Cheddar or Gruyère*
         *1 chopped onion, fried*
           *till transparent*
175 g   *6 oz chopped bacon, fried*
           *till crisp*
         *1 large bunch mixed fresh*
           *herbs–parsley, lemon*
           *balm, tarragon, or*
           *whatever available, chopped*
         *Salt and pepper*

If making the pastry in a Magimix, beat all the ingredients until the pastry balls up; if making by hand, cut flour and butter together with a knife, mix in egg yolk and water, turn out and roll out immediately. Line a greased flan dish and leave in the fridge.*

Mix all the filling ingredients together,* pour into the flan case and bake in a slow oven, 300°F 150°C gas 2, for 1 hour. Sit the flan dish on the bottom of the oven to make sure that the base of the flan is well cooked.

PREPARATION TIME 30 minutes.

*The filling and pastry can be made a day in advance and assembled just before cooking.

Serve with a large bowl of mixed salad, and a chilled white Muscadet or a Blanc de Blancs.

### RHUBARB AND GINGER ICE CREAM

This must be made in advance and frozen.

750 g   *1½ lb rhubarb, chopped*
175 g   *6 oz castor sugar*
275 ml   *½ pint double cream*
125 g   *4 oz crystallized ginger*

#### TUILES D'AMANDES
(see page 22)

or

#### BELGIAN CHOCOLATE
#### BISCUITS
(recipe and ingredients
on page 108)

Shake the rhubarb over a gentle heat until the juices appear, then add the sugar. Cook until soft and purée. Cool. Whip the cream, chop the ginger and fold into the purée mixture. (I often add small broken pieces of meringue which I usually have stored in a tin.) Freeze immediately.

Serve the ice cream in separate glasses and decorate with a twist of orange.

---

# Saturday Lunch in the garden

## continued

**BELGIAN CHOCOLATE BISCUITS**

225 g  *8 oz digestive biscuits and Rich Tea biscuits*
175 g  *6 oz butter*
50 g  *2 oz glacé cherries*
     *2 whole eggs*
225 g  *8 oz plain chocolate*
125 g  *4 oz walnuts, chopped*
     *2 dessertspoons castor sugar*
     *A good slug of Cointreau or Grand Marnier*
     *Zest of 1 orange*

Break up (do not crush) the biscuits. Melt the chocolate and butter separately. Beat the eggs and stir in the melted chocolate, butter and sugar. Add the nuts and cherries and biscuit pieces. Finally add the Cointreau or Grand Marnier and the orange zest. Squash the mixture into a baking tray and put in the fridge until hard. Lift out and cut into squares.

To serve, pile up the biscuits on a plate – a china cake stand is very pretty – and serve with a bowl of whipped cream decorated with orange zest.

# Saturday Dinner

## (for 8 people)

## SCALLOP AND PRAWN PANCAKES WITH TOMATO AND GARLIC SAUCE

### PANCAKES

| | |
|---|---|
| 225 g | *8 oz plain flour* |
| | *3 eggs* |
| 575 ml | *1 pint milk* |

### FILLING

| | |
|---|---|
| 450 g | *1 lb prawns* |
| 450 g | *1 lb baby scallops or queens* |
| 50 g | *2 oz butter* |
| | *1 onion, chopped* |
| | *2 level tablespoons flour* |
| 275 ml | *½ pint water* |
| 150 ml | *¼ pint white wine* |
| 275 ml | *½ pint single cream* |
| | *Fennel* |
| | *Lemon juice to taste* |
| | *Seasoning* |

### TOMATO AND GARLIC SAUCE

| | |
|---|---|
| | *3 cloves of garlic, crushed* |
| 1 kg | *2 lb canned tomatoes or 1 lb fresh and 1 lb canned* |
| | *Olive oil* |
| | *Seasoning* |
| | *A little sugar* |

Make pancakes in advance (see page 153), leaving batter to stand for at least 30 minutes before cooking. Interleafing each pancake with greaseproof, stack, wrap and refrigerate or deep freeze.

Poach the prawns, scallops and the fennel in the water and white wine for 15 minutes. Strain off stock and keep. Melt the butter in a heavy saucepan and cook the onion until transparent. Stir in the flour, off the heat, then cook until smooth. Gradually add the fish stock and cook over a low heat until thick and smooth. Add the cream, continue stirring over a low heat and cook gently for 20 minutes or until the sauce is the right consistency.* Season well, add the shellfish, lemon juice to taste and finally the chopped fennel. Cover this mixture with greaseproof paper until you need it.

An hour or so before dinner fill the pancakes, lay them in a well-greased ovenproof dish, dot with butter and cover the dish with tin foil. Bake in a hot oven, 400°F 200°C gas 6, for 20–30 minutes or until heated through.

PREPARATION TIME 30 minutes.

*Can be made the day before.

Fry the garlic in the oil until pale golden, add tomatoes and seasoning and cook for 15 minutes. Purée and sieve. Serve very hot with the pancakes, in a separate dish.
  Will keep warm.

## ROAST ROLLED SIRLOIN OF BEEF

| | |
|---|---|
| 3 kg | *6 lb rolled sirloin* |
| | *Garlic to taste* |
| | *Butter and olive oil* |

Slash the meat, insert slices of garlic and roast in butter and olive oil. Allow 10 minutes to the lb (450 g) altogether – start off for 20 minutes in a hot oven, 450°F 230°C gas 8, then finish off at a lower temperature, 350°F 180°C gas 4.

# Saturday Dinner

continued

**GREEN HOLLANDAISE
SAUCE**

400 g   *14 oz butter*
*8 egg yolks*
*1 tablespoon cold water*
*Juice of 1 lemon*
*Black pepper*
*Salt (if using unsalted butter)*
*1 large handful of chopped
    parsley and chives or
    marjoram*
*6 small spring onions,
    finely chopped*

**ROAST POTATOES**
(see page 31)

*3 per person*

The addition of the onion to this sauce makes it a little more original,
but not quite a Bernaise sauce.

Melt the butter, add the water and lemon juice and keep warm until
needed.

Beat the yolks with an electric mixer in a heavy saucepan until
really thick; gradually pour the butter mixture on to the yolks and
continue beating all the time off the heat. Finally stand the pot on a
very low heat and continue whisking until thick. Stand in a *bain marie*
of hot water to keep warm until ready to serve. At the last minute stir
in the herbs and spring onions.

**BOILED BROCCOLI**

1¼ kg   *3 lb broccoli*

**BOILED FENNEL**

*10 fennel*

Put into boiling salted water and cook for about 5 minutes. I always
undercook my vegetables: I like them crunchy.

Put into boiling salted water and cook for about 15 minutes.

Drain both vegetables, put into a serving dish, dot with a little
butter and keep warm until needed.

(I have made the quantities for the green vegetables a little on the
generous side, so you have enough left over for Sunday supper soup.)

### PEPPERMINT ROULADE

6 eggs, separated
225 g  8 oz Bourneville chocolate
225 g  8 oz castor sugar
275 ml  ½ pint double cream
Crème de Menthe
½ teaspoon peppermint essence
Icing sugar and burnt flaked almonds to decorate
8 After Eight chocolates

Beat the egg yolks and sugar together until pale cream coloured and thick. Melt the chocolate in the top of a double saucepan with 1 tablespoon of cold water – be careful not to overcook. Then mix the chocolate with the peppermint essence and stir into the yolk and sugar mixture. Beat the egg whites until very stiff and fold into the chocolate mixture.

Line a Swiss roll tin, approximately 10 inches (25 cm) by 12 inches (30 cm) with oiled tin foil. The foil should stand up about 1 inch (2 cm) over the edges of the tin.

Spread the mixture into the tin and bake on the middle rack at 375°F 190°C gas 5 for 15–20 minutes until well risen and cake-like. When cooked remove from oven and allow to get completely cold (on its foil).

Whip the double cream and stir in 1½ tablespoons of Crème de Menthe. Spread this evenly over the chocolate 'cake' and carefully roll it up as a Swiss roll (lift the foil on the long side of the tin and roll away from you, easing the cake off the foil on to a serving dish with the aid of a long knife).*

Finally dust the roulade with sieved icing sugar and scatter with flaked almonds which you have browned under the grill. Decorate down the centre with After Eights cut in half.

Have a large bowl of cherries on the table with the roulade and a bowl of extra whipped peppermint cream.

*This can be made a day in advance and kept in the fridge.

WINES I would serve champagne before dinner, a 1977 Gewürztraminer with the first course, and a 1967 Ducru-Beaucaillou with the main course. The port would be a 1966 Mr Warre.

# Sunday Lunch

(for 6 people)

## CHILLED CARROT AND ORANGE SOUP

This soup is most successful made with a really good chicken stock. The best chicken stock I ever made was with the carcase of a smoked chicken, plus giblets. This obviously may not always be possible, but it is worth remembering.

Sauté the chopped onion, carrot and potato for 10 minutes. Do not brown. Add ½ pint (275 ml) of chicken stock and cook slowly for 30 minutes until all the vegetables are very soft. Liquidize until smooth and while still hot stir in the orange juice and the rest of the stock. Stir in the cream, season and chill. Decorate with mint leaves and orange peel.

This can be made a day or so in advance.

PREPARATION TIME 40 minutes.

| | |
|---|---|
| 1 kg | *2 lb carrots* |
| | *2 medium onions* |
| | *1 small potato* |
| 575 ml | *1 pint good chicken stock* |
| | *Juice of 1–2 oranges, according to taste* |
| 275 ml | *½ pint single cream* |
| | *Seasoning* |

## STUFFED LEG OF VEAL

Mix all the stuffing ingredients together, stuff the veal and sew up the ends (a needle and thread is quite good enough). Roll meat in seasoned flour, then in a beaten egg and finally in toasted bread-crumbs. Roast in a moderate oven, 350°F 180°C gas 4, for about 2 hours (or until cooked through) in a mixture of butter and olive oil. Baste fairly frequently. The outside must be brown and crisp, so if necessary turn up the oven for the last 10 minutes.

| | |
|---|---|
| 4 kg (3 kg boned) | *8 lb of veal (get your butcher to bone it for you), boned weight approximately 6 lb* |

STUFFING

| | |
|---|---|
| 350 g | *12 oz fresh brown breadcrumbs* |
| | *1 medium onion, chopped and softened in butter* |
| 225 g | *8 oz bacon, fried until crisp* |
| 225 g | *8 oz celery, chopped* |
| 125 g | *4 oz walnuts, roughly chopped* |
| 225 g | *8 oz cooking apples, peeled and chopped* |
| | *Salt and pepper* |
| | *Fresh marjoram or origano* |

CRUST

*Seasoned flour*
*3 handfuls toasted white breadcrumbs*
*1 beaten egg*

# Sunday Lunch
## continued

---

**PUREE OF SPINACH**

750 g  *1½ lb spinach*

Cook in butter until soft, about 10 minutes, drain very well and liquidize.

MANGE TOUT Put 1 lb (500 g) tailed *mange tout* in a bowl of iced water to crisp up (this can be done a day in advance) and plunge into boiling salted water for 5–6 minutes.

SAUTE POTATOES Parboil 4 lb (2 kg) potatoes, then chop and fry until golden, about 12–15 minutes, in butter and oil.

My wine would be a 1976 Château La Tour Seguy.

## GOOSEBERRY FOOL

1 kg  *2 lb gooseberries*
275 ml  *½ pint double cream, whipped*
*Rose geranium leaves*

The geranium leaves in this recipe are optional – but I always have a couple of plants in the house. They're particularly nice in the gents!

Cook the gooseberries without any water until soft, then purée in a blender and sweeten to taste. Stir in the cream, roughly chop the geranium leaves and mix in. Decorate with an extra dollop of cream and a geranium leaf on top.

This can be made a couple of days in advance.

PREPARATION TIME 15 minutes.

**FORK BISCUITS**
**(8–12 biscuits)**

125 g  *4 oz butter*
50 g  *2 oz castor sugar*
150 g  *5 oz self-raising flour*
*2–3 drops vanilla*
*essence*

Cream the butter with a wooden spoon. Add the sugar and beat together until white (or use a Magimix). Stir in the flour and vanilla essence. Roll the mixture into balls the size of a walnut. Grease a baking sheet, place the balls on the sheet and flatten with a fork. Bake at 375°F 190°C gas 5 for 7–8 minutes.

These can be made a day or so in advance and stored in an airtight tin.

---

# Sunday Supper by the fire

(for 4 people)

## BROCCOLI AND FENNEL SOUP

Purée the remains of the broccoli and fennel from Saturday dinner, add ¾ pint (425 ml) good strong chicken stock, season to taste and serve with a dollop of whipped cream on each helping.

## SCRAMBLED EGGS WITH BACON AND CROUTONS

225 g    *8 oz streaky bacon*
*3 slices of white bread*
*3 large eggs per person*
*Olive oil*
*Butter*
*Parsley, chopped*

Dice the bacon, fry until crisp, and keep warm. Remove crusts from the bread and cut into small squares.

Fry the croûtons in the bacon fat with a little extra olive oil. Keep hot in the oven with the bacon on a dish lined with kitchen paper. Beat the eggs and scramble in softened butter until only just cooked. Put on a serving dish and sprinkle the bacon and croûtons on top. Dust with parsley.

Finish supper with cheese and fruit.

# Sally Worthington

*Friday*

SUPPER

Tomato Cobb

Lamb Cutlets in Sorrel or Mint and Cream Sauce
New Potatoes
Salad

*Saturday*

LUNCH

Jambon Persillé
Hot Cheese and Herb Bread
Potato Salad and Sour Cream

Manchurian Apple Tart

DINNER

Layered Spinach and Salmon Terrine with Green Mayonnaise

Roast Fillet of Beef and Peppercorn Sauce
Gratin of Courgettes
New Potatoes
French Bean Salad

Strawberry Charlotte

*Sunday*

LUNCH

Cold Loin of Pork with Pistachio Nuts
Kidney Bean and Pasta Salad
Green Salad

Red and Black Fruit Salad

SUPPER

Baked Eggs

Roast Beef Salad

# Friday Supper

(for 6 people)

MAYONNAISE

575 ml
- *1 pint olive oil*
- *1 dessertspoon white wine vinegar*
- *1 teaspoon French mustard*
- *4 egg yolks*
- *Salt*

- *2 tablespoons finely chopped onion or spring onions*
- *20 tomatoes*
- *4 tablespoons mayonnaise*
- *1½–2 teaspoons Worcester sauce*
- *Salt and pepper*
- *Sour cream or whipped cream and chives for garnishing*

- *6 lamb chops or 12 cutlets*
- *Butter and oil*

150 ml
- *¼ pint single cream*
- *2 tablespoons mint or sorrel, chopped*

GREEN SALAD

- *2 hearts of lettuce*
- *½ teaspoon soft brown sugar*
- *1 teaspoon rock salt*
- *Black pepper*
- *1½ tablespoons lemon juice*
- *Small clove of garlic, pressed*
- *Plenty of chopped herbs*
- *6 tablespoons olive oil*

My menu for a June weekend includes lots of cold food that can easily be carried outside.

I make in advance 1 pint (575 ml) of mayonnaise and chop at least 12 tablespoons of parsley, as I use these in small quantities in various recipes. I usually cook Friday supper when guests have arrived so they can sit outside and enjoy the evening first, especially if it has been a hot drive out of London.

Make the mayonnaise: mix the yolks and mustard in a mixer and very slowly add the oil, add vinegar and season.

## TOMATO COBB

This is not a soup but is eaten with a spoon. You can make your own sour cream by just adding lemon juice to some cream and leaving it for about one hour.

Scald the tomatoes, peel and deseed. Just before serving chop them and mix with the onion, mayonnaise, salt, pepper and Worcester sauce. Put into individual bowls and top with sour cream and chopped chives.

All this can be prepared in advance and assembled at the last minute.

## LAMB CUTLETS (OR CHOPS) IN SORREL AND CREAM SAUCE

This is a very light and delicious sauce.

Trim fat from chops or cutlets and fry in a mixture of butter and oil until nicely browned but still pink inside (about 8 minutes). Remove from heat and keep warm. Pour off excess fat. Deglaze pan, in other words, simply add single cream. Season well, bring to the boil and add mint or sorrel.

Serve with boiled new potatoes.

Sprinkle the lettuce with salt, sugar, herbs and pepper. Put in fridge. Mix the rest of the ingredients to make a vinaigrette, and pour over the lettuce just before serving.

Serve this as a separate course with a large piece of Brie.

# Saturday Lunch

## (for 6 people)

---

### JAMBON PERSILLE

| | |
|---|---|
| 1 kg | 2 lb piece of cooked gammon and 1 hambone |
| | or |
| 1½ kg | 3 lb uncooked gammon |
| | ½ glass vermouth |
| | 1 pig's foot |
| 275 ml | ½ pint dry white wine |
| | 2 tablespoons tarragon or wine vinegar |
| | Grated nutmeg |
| | 1 clove crushed garlic |
| | Salt and freshly ground black pepper |
| | 10 tablespoons finely chopped parsley |
| | 2 tablespoons gelatine if needed |

This must be made in advance. You can use cooked gammon, in which case make a stock by simmering a pig's foot and a hambone with an onion, a bay leaf and a few peppercorns for about 2 hours. Alternatively, buy the gammon uncooked, soak it in cold water overnight and then bring slowly to the boil. Simmer for twenty minutes per pound and twenty minutes over. I would soak the gammon over Thursday night and cook it on Friday.

Cut the ham into cubes. Wet a glass bowl and dust with 2 tablespoons of parsley. Put in ham. Allow stock to cook with the pig's foot until syrupy (if you need to use gelatine, soften 2 tablespoons of it in a little hot water and stir into hot stock). When it is on the point of setting, add 8 tablespoons of chopped parsley to stock and pour over ham. Allow to set. I serve from the bowl rather than unmoulding.

### CHEESE AND HERB BREAD

| | |
|---|---|
| 75 g | 3 oz strong Cheddar |
| 225 g | 8 oz self-raising flour |
| | ½ teaspoon salt |
| | 3 tablespoons chopped parsley, chives and marjoram |
| 275 ml | ¼ pint milk |
| | 1 egg |
| | 1 teaspoon Moutarde de Meaux |

Serve with the following bread.

I make this on Saturday morning when the guests are hopefully still in bed.

Mix the Cheddar with the flour and salt, add parsley, chives and marjoram. Mix the milk with the egg and mustard, stir into flour mixture and mix well. Put into a well buttered 1-lb (450-g) loaf tin and cook for 1 hour at 350°F 180°C gas 4.

### POTATO SALAD AND SOUR CREAM DRESSING

| | |
|---|---|
| 1 kg | 2 lb small new potatoes |
| | ½ cucumber cut into matchsticks |
| | 2 tablespoons mayonnaise |
| 275 ml | 1 carton sour cream |
| | 1 teaspoon Moutarde de Meaux |

Use good salad potatoes for this recipe. You can make your own sour cream (see page 129).

Cook the potatoes, cool, add the cucumber matchsticks and cover with the dressing made of mayonnaise, sour cream and mustard mixed together.
    Alternatively cook new potatoes and spring onions in foil with butter and plenty of salt and pepper for approximately 1 hour.

---

### MANCHURIAN APPLE TART

250 g    *8 oz digestive biscuits*
50 g    *2 oz melted butter*
275 ml    *½ pint double cream*
*3 tablespoons coarse marmalade*
*3 apples*
*½ lemon*
*½ orange*
*2 tablespoons Golden Syrup*
*2 tablespoons sultanas*

To make the biscuit flan case, crush digestive biscuits, add melted butter and stir until butter is absorbed. Spread mixture over the bottom of a 9-inch (22-cm) flan tin and cool to harden.*

Whip the cream and fold in marmalade. Spread over biscuit base.

Make a purée of the chopped apples, lemon and orange. Put in pan with Golden Syrup and 3 tablespoons of water. Cook very gently until soft. Cool and put through Mouli or sieve. Fold in the sultanas and top the pudding with the purée.

*These can be prepared separately in advance and assembled at the last minute.

# Saturday Dinner

## (for 8 people)

### LAYERED SPINACH AND SALMON TERRINE

This is an extremely pretty and impressive starter, and it tastes delicious.

To make the Béchamel sauce, melt the butter in a saucepan, add the flour off the heat, return to heat and add the milk slowly.

**BECHAMEL SAUCE**

*2 tablespoons butter*
*1 tablespoon flour*
275 ml · *½ pint milk*
1½ kg *3 lb fresh of frozen spinach*
250 g *8 oz salmon or any trout without bones*
50 g *2 oz softened butter*
*6 tablespoons whipped cream*
*4 egg whites, beaten*
65 g *2½ oz gelatine*
*Seasoning*
*Freshly grated nutmeg*
*4 tablespoons mayonnaise (see Tomato Cobb)*
*1 lemon to garnish*

Put salmon or trout in cold water and bring to the boil. Remove, skin, bone and pound. Mix with Béchamel sauce. Fold in softened butter and 2 tablespoons of whipped cream. Dissolve 1 oz (25 g) of gelatine in 4 tablespoons of water and fold into salmon mixture. Season with salt, pepper and nutmeg. Set aside.

Cook spinach in butter only, drain very well, cool, then purée. Fold in mayonnaise, 1½ oz (40 g) gelatine dissolved in 6 tablespoons of water, 4 tablespoons of whipped cream and stiffly beaten egg whites. Put half the spinach mousse in the bottom of a mould (I use one of those long tins with removable sides as the spinach mousse is not particularly firm in contrast to the firmer fish layer) and leave it in the fridge to set. Then add all the salmon mousse and top with the rest of the spinach mousse.

To serve, turn out and decorate with thinly sliced lemon. I serve this with a bowl of mayonnaise thinned with a little white wine or vermouth and coloured with chopped herbs (see page 116).

### FILLET OF BEEF AND PEPPERCORN SAUCE

GREEN PEPPERCORN
SAUCE

*1 small onion or shallot*
75 g   *3 oz mushrooms, finely sliced*
150 ml   *¼ pint vermouth*
*1 tablespoon tomato purée*
*1 tablespoon green peppercorns*
*Salt and pepper*
*Oil and butter*
425 ml   *¾ pint demi-glace sauce*

DEMI-GLACE SAUCE
(enough for 2 pints/1 litre)

50 g   *2 oz diced carrots*
50 g   *2 oz diced onions*
50 g   *2 oz diced celery*
50 g   *2 oz diced bacon*
*6 tablespoons cooking oil*
50 g   *2 oz flour*
*3 pints good brown stock*
*2 tablespoons tomato purée*
*Bouquet garni*
*1 tablespoon mushrooms,*
  *chopped*
*Salt and pepper*

If you use a whole fillet of beef you will have enough to eat cold on Sunday. Cook it in a hot oven, 450°F 230°C gas 8, in dripping for 10 minutes per lb (450 g).

Chop onions or shallots and sauté in butter and oil until barely coloured. Add mushrooms and cook for a few minutes. Add vermouth and boil until reduced to 1 tablespoon. Stir in tomato purée and demi-glace sauce. Simmer for 5 minutes and add green peppercorns. Adjust seasoning and just before serving stir in 1 oz (25 g) softened butter.

PREPARATION TIME 15 minutes, having previously made the demi-glace sauce.

SIMPLE METHOD Cook vegetables and bacon slowly for about 10 minutes in oil. Blend in flour and cook, stirring, until golden brown. Remove from heat, add tomato purée and blend in boiling stock. Add bouquet garni. Simmer, partially covered, for about 2 hours. Skim from time to time. If it gets too thick thin with a little more stock.

Strain, pressing the juice out of the vegetables. Season and degrease. I freeze this and use it as required.

# Saturday Dinner

## continued

---

### GRATIN OF COURGETTES

275 ml

*8 medium courgettes*
*½ pint double cream*
*1 egg*
*3 rounded tablespoons
  grated Gruyère*
*Salt and pepper*

Cut the courgettes into diagonal slices and blanch in boiling water, about 2 minutes, keeping them slightly crunchy. Put into gratin dish. Mix together the cream, egg and 2 tablespoons of Gruyère, season and pour over courgettes. Dot with butter and bake in hot oven for 10 minutes.

The courgettes can be chopped and the sauce made in advance and assembled just before heating.

This is also delicious with the addition of flaked chicken and a handful of breadcrumbs as either a lunch dish or Sunday supper dish.

NEW POTATOES boiled in their skins (about 2 lb – 1 kg)

### FRENCH BEAN SALAD

1 kg

*2 lb French beans*

Barely cook the beans (about 5 minutes in boiling salted water) then top with roughly chopped tomatoes, skinned and seeded, a little finely chopped spring onion and basil and not too harsh a vinaigrette.

## STRAWBERRY CHARLOTTE

1 kg *2 lb strawberries*
75 g *4 boxes sponge fingers*
225 g *8 oz unsalted butter*
150 g *6 oz castor sugar*
150 g *6 oz ground almonds*
425 ml *¾ pint lightly whipped cream*
275 ml *½ pint Cointreau*

Line the base of an ungreased 3-pint (1½-litre) charlotte mould with greaseproof paper. Beat butter with castor sugar until pale and fluffy. Beat in half the Cointreau and then ground almonds. Fold in cream. Mix together the remaining Cointreau with ¼ pint (150 ml) water. Dip sponge fingers into this and line sides of mould.

Turn one third of the almond cream into lined mould, cover with a layer of strawberries, pointed ends down and pushed well into the the cream. Then cover with another layer of dipped sponge fingers. Repeat, ending with almond cream. Trim off any sponge fingers standing up and press into top of cream. Cover with greaseproof paper and a saucer weighted down and leave overnight. This must be well chilled. Turn out and decorate with whipped cream and whole strawberries.

Can be made on Friday.

PREPARATION TIME 30 minutes.

### STRAWBERRY SAUCE

500 g *1 lb strawberries, frozen
  or fresh*
225 g *8 oz icing sugar*
*Lemon juice*

On another occasion without so many preceding sauces I might make a strawberry sauce with this.

Sieve the strawberries (if using frozen ones make sure they are well drained). I put mine through a Mouli. Beat in the sugar until it has dissolved and add a squeeze of lemon juice to taste.

---

# Sunday Lunch

## (for 6 people)

---

## COLD LOIN OF PORK WITH PISTACHIO NUTS

| | |
|---|---|
| 1¼ kg | 2½ lb loin of pork |
| 25 g | 1 oz pistachio nuts |
| | Ground black pepper |
| | Chopped herbs |
| 250 ml | ⅓ pint dry white wine |
| 275 ml | ½ pint water |

Get the butcher to bone and skin the pork and keep the scraps. Make little slits in the fat and press in shelled pistachio nuts all over in a neat pattern. Sprinkle inside of meat with ground black pepper and herbs (parsley and lemon thyme or rosemary). Roll meat and tie neatly. Put it into a deep pot with the bones and skin tucked in around the joint. Pour in the white wine and water. Cook in a preheated oven, 350°F 180°C gas 4, until fat is coloured, then cover tightly with foil and lid, reduce heat to 300°F 150°C gas 2 and cook for a further 2 hours.

Remove the skin and bones and leave the meat to cool in the juice. This will set to a lovely jelly. Carefully remove the fat, chop the jelly and arrange it round the meat on a serving dish. Or simply slice the meat and serve it on a bed of parsley. Serve with a good brown bread.

The dripping from this joint is delicious for those who like it, spread it on bread.

### KIDNEY BEAN AND PASTA SALAD

| | |
|---|---|
| 400 g | 14 oz tin red kidney beans |
| | Grated rind and juice of 1 lemon |
| | 1 small clove of garlic, crushed |
| | A few basil leaves or 1 tablespoon parsley |
| | Salt and freshly ground black pepper |
| 275 ml | ½ pint olive oil |
| | Sesame seeds |
| | A handful of pasta shells per person |

Boil pasta shells till just cooked. Put the lemon, garlic, parsley or basil into a Magimix or liquidizer, switch on and pour in olive oil until a lovely thick green liquid is arrived at. Pour over pasta while still warm and add beans. Before serving garnish with sesame seeds.

This sauce discolours so do not make it too far in advance.

The alternative would be a lentil salad made from whole grey (not split yellow) lentils cooked until soft, mixed with chives and dressed with half yogurt and half sour cream. Season well.

## RED AND BLACK FRUIT SALAD

| | |
|---|---|
| 500 g | 1 lb raspberries |
| ,, | 1 lb strawberries |
| ,, | 1 lb redcurrants |
| ,, | 1 lb white currants (if you can get them) |
| 250 g | 8 oz blackcurrants (or blackberries) |

This is a very good pudding for those who do not have enough of any one fruit in the garden for a dish on its own.

I make this in a large glass bowl. Arrange layers of raspberries, a few strawberries and lots of redcurrants alternately with a few blackcurrants or blackberries. Go lightly on these or they will overpower the rest of the fruit. If you are lucky enough to have white currants these are best of all.

Make a sugar syrup of ⅛ pint (75 ml) water and 4 tablespoons castor sugar. Cool slightly and pour over the fruit.

I do not chill this salad but if possible leave it on a sunny windowsill to draw out the juices. I would not serve it with cream but Cœur à la Crème or Fromage Blanc or petit Suisse cheeses.

---

# Sunday Supper

## (for 2 people)

### BAKED EGGS

Cook eggs in ramekins with cream mixed with a little Moutarde de Meaux. Alternatively put a layer of finely sliced Gruyère in bottom of pots, break in the eggs and top with seasoned cream.

Put in hot oven, 450°F 230°C gas 8, in *bain marie* or bowl of water for 10 minutes or until just set.

### ROAST BEEF SALAD

Cut cold roast beef left over from Saturday night into strips and mix with vinaigrette, chives and capers. Pile in centre of plate and surround with sliced salad potatoes and quarters of tomatoes.

If I were not serving the egg dish first I might add halves of hard-boiled eggs if necessary to eke out the beef.

# JULY

----◄◇►----

## Antoinette Parkes

*Kimbridge was originally a mill house,
but it was enlarged and completely altered
in 1865, and again in 1912; and it
is this Edwardian building of red brick under
a tiled roof, complete with characteristic
details including a stained glass window and a
verandah, which now remains. Sadly the
architect is unknown.*

**Friday**

SUPPER

Courgette Soup

Scallops in White Wine Sauce
Prawn Salad
Baby New Potatoes

Hot Bread and Brie

**Saturday**

LUNCH

Tomatoes and Fresh Basil in Vinaigrette Dressing

Onion Quiche
Spinach, Courgette and Bacon Salad

Fresh Cherries

DINNER

Melon, Mint and Grapes in Sour Cream

Lambs Kidneys in Sherry Sauce
Carrots
New Potatoes

Cheese Savouries

Substitute Saturday Night Pudding

**Sunday**

LUNCH

Roast Chicken with Tarragon Sauce
New Potatoes
French Beans

Summer Pudding

SUPPER

Avocado Soup

Dauphine Potatoes
Salad

Cheese

# Friday Supper

## (for 6 people)

### COURGETTE SOUP

| | |
|---|---|
| 1 kg | 2 lb courgettes |
| 850 ml | 1½ pints chicken stock or Knorr chicken cube |
| | Garlic salt |
| 150 ml | ¼ pint cream |
| | Salt |

Slice courgettes quite thinly. Place in chicken stock and cook for about 7 minutes. Purée in blender until very smooth.* Add cream and seasonings. Reheat and serve.

PREPARATION TIME 10 minutes.

*This can be done a day or so in advance.

### SCALLOPS IN WHITE WINE SAUCE

| | |
|---|---|
| 1 kg | 18 fresh scallops (or 2 lb frozen) |
| 175 g | 6 oz thickly sliced button mushrooms |
| | 4 tablespoons butter |
| | 2 tablespoons flour |
| 85 ml | ⅛ pint white wine |
| 425 ml | ¾ pint milk |
| | 2 tablespoons grated Cheddar |
| | 1 tablespoon grated Gruyère |
| | 2 tablespoons cream |
| | Salt and pepper |

Melt 3 tablespoons of butter and blend in the flour off the heat. Add the milk, cheeses and simmer for 5 minutes. Add the wine, seasonings and cream.*

Half an hour before the meal, sauté the mushrooms in the remaining butter for about 1 minute. Wash the scallops and put in boiling salted water for 1 minute. Drain very well and put in baking dish. Add mushrooms to sauce and pour over scallops. Put in hot oven for 10 minutes while you are eating the first course.

*I do this in the morning or day before and cover with cling film.

Serve with baby new potatoes cooked in their skins and with the prawn salad.

### PRAWN SALAD

2–3 good lettuce heads
1 tablespoon dill leaves
12 fresh whole prawns
1 bunch spring onions

I usually wash lettuce in cold water well in advance and keep it in a plastic bag in fridge.

Mix everything together with a dressing of 1 tablespoon tarragon vinegar to 4 tablespoons olive oil, 1 rounded teaspoon French mustard and salt and pepper.

HOT BREAD AND BRIE If you buy Brie that is chalky inside, scrape the top and sides with a fork. This allows the cheese to breathe. (The skin will turn brown.)

# Saturday Lunch

(for 6 people)

## TOMATOES AND FRESH BASIL IN VINAIGRETTE DRESSING

*12 large tomatoes or 16 small ones*
*15 whole fresh basil leaves*
*1 tablespoon chopped fresh basil leaves*
100 g *12 thin slices (4 oz) Mozarella cheese*
*4 tablespoons green olive oil*
*1 tablespoon white wine vinegar*
*Salt and pepper*

Skin and quarter the tomatoes. Cut the cheese into thin slices. Toss the tomatoes in the vinaigrette, add the chopped basil.

Arrange slices of cheese around the edge of 9-inch (22-cm) flan dish, pile tomatoes in the centre, decorate with the whole basil leaves.

PREPARATION TIME 7 minutes.

## ONION QUICHE

SHORTCRUST PASTRY

350 g *12 oz flour*
115 g *4½ oz margarine*
40 g *1½ oz lard*
*5 tablespoons ice-cold water*
*1 teaspoon salt*

FILLING

*2 Spanish onions*
*5 tablespoons butter*
*1 tablespoon flour*
*3 eggs*
275 ml *½ pint cream*
*Salt and freshly ground pepper*

Make the pastry. I make mine in a Magimix. Sift the flour and salt, add the margarine and lard in chunks and mix till breadcrumbs. Add water. Make a ball of dough. Wrap it in greaseproof paper and put it in the fridge for half an hour. Roll out and line a 9-inch (22-cm) flan dish. Prick the bottom.*

Bake blind for 10 minutes. Leave to cool for ¼ hour.

Chop the onions finely; soften in butter, cool, add flour, eggs, cream and mix well. Season to taste.* Pour into pastry shell and cook in hot oven, 450°F 230°C gas 8, for ½ hour.

*This can be done a day in advance.

# Saturday Lunch
## continued

**SPINACH, COURGETTE AND BACON SALAD**

*1 large handful of fresh*
*spinach*
*3 small or 2 large courgettes*
*3 rashers of bacon with*
*rinds removed*
*4 tablespoons olive oil*
*1 tablespoon white wine*
*vinegar*
*Salt and pepper*
*1 teaspoon French mustard*

When I buy or pick fresh spinach I wash and trim it and put it in a polythene bag in the fridge to stay crisp.

Shred spinach. Grill bacon till crispy, then crumble. Cut the skin off the courgettes, with a very small layer of flesh. Discard insides and cut skin into matchsticks. Mix everything together and add vinaigrette. Toss well.

Large bowl of black cherries for pudding.

# Saturday Dinner

## (for 8 people)

### MELON, MINT AND GRAPES IN SOUR CREAM

6 small Charantaise melons
(or 2 large sweet melons)
275 ml   Scant ½ pint double cream
Juice of ½ lemon
2 tablespoons chopped mint
500 g   1 lb seedless grapes

This dessert has a very refreshing and original taste. It can be made a day in advance and kept in the refrigerator.

Make balls of melon using melon scoop. Mix the lemon with the cream until it turns sour and leave for ½ hour out of fridge. Wash the grapes and remove stems. Chop the mint, add it to grapes and the sour cream and put in the balls of melon. Mix well. Serve in individual glass bowls.

PREPARATION TIME 10 minutes.

### LAMBS' KIDNEYS IN SHERRY SAUCE

18 lambs' kidneys
40 g   1½ oz butter
1 tablespoon chopped parsley
250 g   9 oz mushrooms (optional)
25 g   1 oz butter (optional)

SAUCE

40 g   1½ oz flour
40 g   1½ oz butter
150 ml   ¼ pint chicken or veal stock
6 tablespoons sherry

De-core kidneys (I find butchers rarely do this properly) by cutting in half and removing core with a pair of scissors.* Season with salt and pepper. Heat the butter in a frying pan and cook the kidneys over a gentle heat for 2–3 minutes on either side until they become firm and turn colour. Lift out of pan, put in a dish, cover and keep warm.

To make the sauce melt the butter and blend in the flour off the heat. Return to heat and cook for a few minutes, add the stock and bring to the boil, stirring constantly. Cook for 4–5 minutes. Add the sherry and season to taste. Cook for a few minutes.* Add the kidneys and arrange on a serving dish. Keep warm. Garnish with chopped parsley.

The mushrooms, sliced and sautéed in an ounce of butter, may be added as a finish to this dish.

COOKING TIME 5 minutes.

*The kidneys can be de-cored and the sauce prepared a day in advance.

CARROTS

1 kg   2 lb carrots
50 g   2 oz butter
Salt and pepper
Chopped parsley

Slice the carrots very thinly. Heat the butter in a frying pan and cook the carrots for about 2 minutes. Put into dish with all the butter, cover and keep warm. On the point of serving sprinkle on chopped parsley.

Serve with new potatoes boiled in their skins.

### CHEESE SAVOURIES

These savouries are very rich and two per person is usually plenty.

*16 slices white bread*
*16 heaped teaspoons grated*
 *Cheddar*
*Butter*

With a 2-inch (5-cm) round cutter, cut 2 rounds from each slice of bread. Butter them and put 1 heaped teaspoon of cheese on one round and put another round on top like a sandwich. Fry gently in butter until golden on each side. Keep warm until needed. Serve with English mustard.

I make up the sandwiches the day before and leave them in the fridge covered with cling film, then cook them ½ hour before guests arrive and keep in warmer until required.

### SUBSTITUTE SATURDAY NIGHT PUDDING

If for some reason I have not been able to prepare all the food, I can always get home-made ice cream out of the deep freeze. This is usually rhubarb, gooseberry or blackcurrant, because these are the fruits I have in my garden. When I drain rhubarb or blackcurrant after cooking I save the juice and sweeten and chill it as a drink for children, who adore it.

For 6 people:

500 g   *1 lb fruit*
 65 g   *2½ oz castor sugar*
        *4 tablespoons water*
        *3 egg yolks*
275 ml  *½ pint whipped double cream*

Cook the fruit in a little water until it is soft, drain, liquidize until smooth and add the cream. Put the sugar and water in a saucepan, boil rapidly until it forms a thread; remove from the heat and cool slightly, pour on to the egg yolks, whisking all the time until the mixture is thick and pale (use a hand electric beater). Mix with fruit purée and freeze.

# Sunday Lunch

(for 6 people)

## CHICKEN AND TARRAGON

2–2¼ kg · 4–5 lb fresh chicken
3 tablespoons tarragon
leaves, chopped
4 tablespoons butter
275 ml · ½ pint double cream
Salt and pepper
1 tablespoon flour

This is one of the easiest and most delicious ways of cooking chicken.

Work 2 tablespoons butter with 1 tablespoon chopped tarragon and season. Stuff the chicken with the butter mixture and melt 1 good tablespoon of butter in a casserole dish large enough to hold the chicken. Lay the chicken down on its side, cover and cook for 20 minutes to the lb (450 g) in a hot oven, 400°F 200°C gas 6, turning the chicken over halfway through and basting with the butter. When it is cooked, remove it on to a serving dish and keep warm.

Strain some of the butter away so you have about a tablespoon left. Mix this with the flour to a smooth paste. When it is amalgamated, add the cream and the rest of the tarragon. Bring to the boil and when it has thickened pour over the chicken or serve separately in a jug.

SERVE WITH new potatoes garnished with chopped parsley, and French beans cooked in boiling salted water with a dash of lemon juice or bicarbonate of soda to keep their colour, for 6 minutes.

## SUMMER PUDDING

1 kg · 2 lb redcurrants
500 g · 1 lb raspberries
6 thin slices
white bread
3 tablespoons
castor sugar

This traditional pudding should be made at least a day in advance to allow all the juices to be soaked up by the bread.

Stew the redcurrants, stems and all, in a pan with very little water (just to keep them from sticking) until soft, about 6 minutes. Sieve. Add castor sugar to taste.

Cut the crusts off the bread and line a 6-inch (15-cm) pudding bowl, reserving one slice for the top. Fill with one-third of the redcurrant juice, half the raspberries, one-third of the redcurrant juice and the rest of the raspberries. Put the reserved slice of bread on top and a weighted plate on top of that. When cool put in refrigerator to chill.

When ready to serve loosen around the edges with a knife and turn on to a plate. Pour the last third of the redcurrant juice over the top. Serve with a large bowl of whipped cream.

# Sunday Supper

## (for 2 people)

### AVOCADO PEAR SOUP

*1 packet Knorr Chicken*
*Noodle Soup*
*1 avocado*
275 ml *½ pint cream*

Don't be put off by the packet soup in this recipe: it tastes very good. And it is extremely quick to make.

Prepare the packet soup with 1 pint (550 ml) of water only. Chop up the avocado pear, add to the soup, and liquidize together until very smooth. Cool, add the cream, chill and serve.

This should be eaten as soon as it is thoroughly chilled – about 2 hours – otherwise it will turn brown. If you want to make it in the morning add a squeeze of lemon.

### DAUPHINE POTATOES

*4 medium potatoes*
25 g *1 oz butter*
75 ml *⅛ pint water*
40 g *1½ oz plain flour*
*2 eggs, beaten*
*Salt and pepper*
*Nutmeg*
*1 tablespoon grated Cheddar*

These are simply delicious and I think best eaten only with a salad, but if you must a lamb cutlet or cold meat is all they require.

Boil the potatoes until they are soft. In a saucepan melt the butter, then add the water and boil for a couple of minutes, add the flour through a sieve and continue to stir until it thickens; lower the heat and go on stirring until you have a smooth mixture, about 3 minutes. Remove from heat and add the eggs. (If you have a food processor put the egg mixture with the cooked potatoes in it and mix until really smooth.) Purée the potatoes and blend them into the egg mixture a little at a time until it is very smooth. Season with salt, pepper and a little grated nutmeg. Add the cheese.*

TO COOK Into a deep pan of hot oil drop teaspoons of the mixture, cooking about 6–8 at a time. Turn them over very gently, and as soon as they have become a deep golden colour lift them out and put on a hot plate.

These should be served at once: if you cook too many the early ones go mushy, so try to limit the number of people to about 4.

*Can be prepared well in advance.

# Margaret Read

Margaret has a large farmhouse kitchen with huge dresser which is piled with china and bowls of home-made cream made in an extremely ancient electric cream machine.

'The worst thing about a cooking is first thinking of the meals—then the shopping. I thoroughly enjoy cooking for a dinner party, but honestly dislike everyday cooking. I feel I am a cook with very little grace as it bores me rigid so much of the time.'

Her dislike of routine cooking may well be the reason why Margaret is such an original cook.

'I love very fresh, simple food and on the whole don't like sauces, which I often find are too rich and spoil the flavour of the food. I think about my menus and read cookery books a great deal. I only cook puddings for dinner parties and then I would still rather have a savoury.

'I am a great market shopper. Salisbury has a marvellous one on Tuesday and I always buy my fruit and fish there (fruit lasts until the weekend); otherwise it is Waitrose or Marks and Spencers, and the vegetable garden. I might buy a few convenient luxury items in London like Parma ham, or smoked sprats for Sunday supper (unbelievably delicious with hot buttered toast) but rarely make a special trip. I do, however, buy tins of olive oil in London, as I cannot find really good oils in the country. I definitely think that best quality ingredients make all the difference and I never use corn oils or margarine.

'I have recently discovered Rioja, a red or white Spanish wine, which I find is very good value and which I buy from Sherston Wine Company, Malmesbury, Wiltshire.

'I will often try out a brand new recipe at a weekend – and it may be a total disaster! I never cook before Thursday. On Friday morning I finish any shopping I haven't managed to do in the market, but I do try to get everything done before people arrive. In the summer I buy French cheeses, which I love, but in the autumn I buy a whole large Cheddar and just before Christmas a Stilton.

'With the exception of pork, the meat is my own. We are great offal eaters: it is delicious and economical. I often cook it for lunch.'

Margaret always cooks a good breakfast on Saturday morning – particularly if guests are going shooting. This might be fried bread, sausages, bacon, fried eggs or kippers if she can get good fresh ones. On Sunday morning breakfast is a boiled egg, and there is always a large jug of fresh orange juice, home-made marmalade and fresh bread.

'I have an excellent baker in Salisbury so I don't make my own bread. I do make marmalade, but not jam as we never eat it. I don't have a Magimix, but have most gadgets on the Kenwood. I grow all my herbs and vegetables; seakale is ideal to have in the garden as it is always there in the winter. I only freeze surplus vegetables. I freeze soups and pre-cooked nursery foods for the holidays, as well as casseroles, cottage pies and cakes.'

# FISHING WEEKEND

**Friday**

SUPPER

Cassoulette des Champignons

Baked Gammon with Mustard Glaze
New Potatoes
Spinach

Anchovy Crème

**Saturday**

LUNCH

Salad Niçoise
Stilton Quiche

Fresh Fruit

DINNER

Cold uncooked Tomato Soup

Hot Salmon with Hollandaise Sauce
New Potatoes
Peas
Cucumber and Dill Salad

Raspberries and Cream

**Sunday**

LUNCH

Roast Lamb with Parsley and Rosemary
Mint and Orange Sauce
Baby Carrots
Baby Broad Beans

Gooseberry Pie and Cream

SUPPER

Melon
Oeufs en Cocotte

# Friday Supper

## CASSOULETTE DES CHAMPIGNONS

½ kg    *1 lb very small mushrooms*
       *Butter*
150 ml   *¼ pint double cream*
       *Juice of ½ lemon*

Sauté mushrooms very quickly in foaming butter for about one minute. Drain on kitchen paper and sprinkle with salt and pepper. Divide equally in six ramekin dishes.

Mix the cream and lemon juice, using just enough lemon juice to make the cream turn sour. Pour this over the mushrooms (do not put too much cream with the mushrooms or the mixture will be too rich – about one-third full).* Just before serving pop in a very hot oven, 425°F 220°C gas 7, until the cream is bubbling.

*All this can be done in the morning before guests arrive.

## BAKED GAMMON WITH MUSTARD GLAZE

2½–2¼ kg   *5–6 lb boned gammon*
         *joint*
         *Peppercorns*
         *1 tablespoon demerara*
          *sugar*
         *1 bay leaf*

GLAZE

150 g   *6 oz demerara sugar*
       *Juice of a lemon*
       *Zest of orange and juice*
       *2 tablespoons water*
       *2 tablespoons made*
        *mustard*

If you use smoked gammon for this recipe you will need to soak it overnight first. If the gammon is green soak it for one hour in cold water. The gammon should cook altogether for 20 minutes per lb (450 g) and 20 minutes over, two-thirds of the time simmering, one-third baking at 375°F 190°C gas 5.

Put the gammon, peppercorns, bay leaf and sugar in a large saucepan. Cover with cold water, bring gently to the boil and simmer for required time.

Meanwhile prepare the glaze. Cook all the ingredients over a low heat until sugar has dissolved, then cook rapidly to a thin syrup.

Remove the skin from the gammon, place in a roasting tin, score the fat and baste with the glaze. Bake in oven, 350°F 180°C gas 4, for the remaining one-third of the time, basting frequently. Finally remove joint from oven, pour off excess fat and use juices for a sauce. I simply add enough flour to soak up the fat and then some of the spinach water. Serve with new potatoes and spinach.

## ANCHOVY CREME

150 ml   *¼ pint double cream*
       *2 teaspoons anchovy essence*
       *6 slices of white bread with*
        *crusts removed*
       *Olive oil*
       *12 anchovy fillets, rolled*
       *Chopped parsley, pepper*

Whip the cream with the anchovy essence and season with pepper. Fry small squares of bread in olive oil and dry on kitchen paper (these can be left to keep warm). Just before serving spread the cream mixture on bread and garnish with rolls of anchovies and chopped parsley.

# Saturday Lunch

(for 6 people)

If it is a nice day for fishing I pack all this up
and take it down to the river.

## SALAD NICOISE

200 g   *2 tins of tuna fish*
50 g   *1 tin of anchovy fillets*
*2 heads of lettuce*
*4 tomatoes, quartered*
*3 hard-boiled eggs,*
   *sliced*

This is very much my own version; I often throw in anything I can find on the spur of the moment, so long as it is varied and colourful. With it I serve a hot French stick full of herb butter.

Reserve the oil from the tinned fish. Mix it all together in a large bowl and cover with a vinaigrette dressing made from oils from tuna and anchovies and 2 tablespoons of olive oil, 4 tablespoons of lemon juice, 1 dessertspoon of sugar, 1 dessertspoon of mustard powder, salt and pepper, 1 good tablespoon of chopped mint and thyme.

HERB BREAD Slice a French stick into portions, not quite cutting through the bottom, and fill with butter made from 8 oz (225 g) soft butter mixed with a tablespoon each of thyme, parsley or any fresh herbs you have in the garden. Wrap in tin foil and heat through. (Keep wrapped if going to the river.)

## STILTON QUICHE

225–250 g   *8–9 oz Stilton*
   *(including crust)*
*6 eggs*
*3 tablespoons cream*
*6 green heads of spring*
   *onions*
*Salt and pepper*

SHORTCRUST PASTRY

125–150 g   *5–6 oz mixed butter*
   *and lard*
225 g   *8 oz flour*
*1 egg*
*½ teaspoon salt*

This is excellent hot or cold and freezes well.

Make the pastry.* Line and pre-cook a 9-inch (22-cm) flan dish.
   Mix Stilton, eggs, cream and spring onions altogether in a liquidizer, add salt and pepper.* Pour into pastry case and cook for ½ hour at 350°F 180°C gas 4.

PREPARATION TIME 20 minutes   COOKING TIME 30 minutes.

*Can be prepared separately in advance and assembled at the last minute.

Serve fresh fruit afterwards.

# Saturday Dinner

## (for 8 people)

---

### COLD UNCOOKED TOMATO SOUP

1¾ kg  *4 lb skinned ripe tomatoes*
37 g  *1½ oz castor sugar*
*4 teaspoons salt*
*Juice and zest of a lemon*
*Juice of a medium onion*
275 ml  *½ pint double cream*

Blend tomatoes in liquidizer and sieve to remove pips. Mix thoroughly with all the other ingredients, stirring in the cream last. Chill in fridge.

PREPARATION TIME 15 minutes.

### HOT SALMON WITH HOLLANDAISE SAUCE

3½–5 g  *7–10 lb salmon*
*Lemon juice*
*Salt and pepper*
*Parsley*

Melt some butter and brush it onto a large piece of tin foil and inside the fish. Add a squeeze of lemon juice, salt and pepper and some snips of parsley. Wrap the fish in the foil and bake in a moderate oven, 350°F 180°C gas 4, for approximately 40 minutes. It is the thickness, not the length, of the fish that counts. Remove from the oven when just undercooked if you are keeping it warm. (As long as it is wrapped in foil it continues to cook.)

HOLLANDAISE SAUCE

*3 egg yolks*
*Juice of 2 lemons*
*1 tablespoon water*
425 g  *15 oz butter*

Take the eggs, lemon juice, water and 5 oz (150 g) butter, put in the top of a double saucepan and stir over hot but *not* boiling water until butter has melted. Gradually add a further 10 oz (275 g) butter and the sauce will thicken like mayonnaise.

This can be made 2–3 hours before dinner and will not curdle if kept warm in the double saucepan on top of stove (an Aga is perfect).

With the salmon serve fresh peas and new potatoes.

CUCUMBER AND DILL SALAD Slice a cucumber thinly and sprinkle with fresh dill and a little white wine vinegar poured over just to flavour.

Follow with 4 lb (1¾ kg) raspberries served in a large bowl with a jug of cream; and then a selection of French cheeses.

---

# Sunday Lunch

## (for 6 people)

### ROAST LAMB

Depending on the number of people we have a shoulder or leg and *always* English lamb.

I pierce the skin all over and put in sprigs of parsley. Have plenty of fresh rosemary in the pan and sprinkle the joint with castor sugar and pepper. Cook in a roasting oven, 475°F 240°C gas 9 for 15 minutes per pound (450 g) and then keep warm in simmering oven (or a warmer in an electric oven).

ORANGE AND MINT SAUCE Chop a large handful of mint leaves finely and mix with the juice of an orange, instead of vinegar, and 1 tablespoon of demerara sugar.

BABY BROAD BEANS AND CARROTS Put the vegetables into boiling salted water till just cooked (about 5 minutes) depending on the freshness and size of the vegetables. When cooked sprinkle with chopped parsley and chives.

### GOOSEBERRY PIE

750 g   *1½ lb gooseberries*
125 g   *4 oz demerara sugar*
        *One-third tin of light ale*
125 g   *4 oz icing sugar*
        *1 egg white*

SHORTCRUST PASTRY (use the same recipe as for the Stilton Quiche, page 137).

Prepare the gooseberries and put in dish. Sprinkle with demerara sugar and add the ale. Cover with shortcrust pastry and bake in the oven at 475°F 240°C gas 9, for 15 minutes. Remove and spread the crust with a mixture of icing sugar and well beaten egg white. Return to baking oven, 375°F 190°C gas 5, for a further 10 minutes while you are eating the main course.

# Sunday Supper

## (for 2 people)

Any melon in season. Followed by
### OEUFS EN COCOTTE

Butter one ramekin dish per person. Break in egg and season with salt and pepper. Place in a frying pan gently simmering with water. Add some cream to each dish and cook until set, about 10 minutes. You just have to stick a knife in to test it.

If guests want any more food they raid the larder.

*Caroline Hulse's house in Hampshire
used to be a mill. Red brick under
a tiled roof, it was completely rebuilt
in the 1960s; but the mill wheel still stands
over the stream in the garden.*

# AUGUST

## Caroline Hulse

Caroline Hulse is a superb cook and is excessively modest. She lives in a beautiful little mill house with a stream running through an enchanting garden: honey-suckles, clematis and roses pour over all the walls and trees.

Her kitchen is small and she uses an electric cooker. She has a Magimix and only recently acquired a deep freeze which she uses very sparingly: fruits and purées seem to be all it holds.

'I prepare as much as I can in advance, but I never freeze dishes. I shop on Thursday or Friday and cook just before the meal. I try to pick the vegetables or fruit from the garden just before I am going to cook them, as young vegetables lose so much moisture if picked hours before being eaten. I am always trying out new recipes – I seem to forget the old ones.'

I have never had the same dish twice in Caroline's house. Her food has a very delicate flavour.

'I test my food all the way through the cooking, and find I do not often stick strictly to a recipe. I have found it very hard to prepare these menus, as I had no idea of quantities, or really quite how I made each dish. I add a bit of this and that as I go along. I do not mind having people in the kitchen, but it is really too small to have many. I grow most of my own vegetables, herbs and fruit, and base my menus on what is available.'

Breakfast at Caroline's house, if you're lucky enough to be female, is usually a tray in bed with toast and marmalade. For the men it's down-stairs – eggs and bacon cooked deliciously *sur le plat*. There's always freshly ground coffee, or tea if preferred.

Caroline's everyday white wine would be Blanc de Blanc Mocbaril, and the red 1975 Pavillon, both of which are available from Turle wine vaults in Oxford. For a dinner party she would choose a particularly good claret, such as 1973 Château la Lagune.

Caroline's recipes are very simple to follow, and all are quite delicious.

*Friday*

SUPPER

Cold Cucumber Soup

Fish Pudding
Green Salad with Hot Butter Dressing

Cambozala or Cheddar Cheese

*Saturday*

LUNCH

Crûdités with Mayonnaise

Cheese Tart
Salad

DINNER

Stuffed Tomatoes
Brown Rolls

Fillet of Beef with Wine Butter
Carrots
Courgettes
Pancake of Potatoes

Green Fruit Salad

*Sunday*

LUNCH

Artichokes

Chicken and Almond Sauce
Potatoes cooked in Butter and Breadcrumbs

Blackcurrant Fool

# Friday Supper

(for 6 people)

## COLD CUCUMBER SOUP

| | |
|---|---|
| | *1 cucumber* |
| 275 ml | *½ pint single cream* |
| 125 ml | *4 fluid oz sour cream* |
| 275 ml | *½ pint good chicken stock* |
| | *1½ teaspoons curry powder* |
| | *Chopped chives for garnishing* |
| | *Salt* |

Chop cucumber in half. Peel one half. Chop both halves roughly and blend in a liquidizer with the cream, chicken stock and sour cream. Add curry powder and salt to taste. Chill.* Garnish with chopped chives. Serve with Melba toast.

PREPARATION TIME 10 minutes.

*This can be made a day in advance.

## FISH PUDDING

| | |
|---|---|
| | *2 pots of potted shrimps* |
| 500 g | *2 lb smoked haddock* |
| 500 g | *1 lb fresh haddock* |
| 750 g | *1½ lb mashed potatoes* |
| 850 ml | *1¼ pints milk* |
| 100 g | *4 oz Cheddar* |
| | *2 good tablespoons butter* |
| | *2 good tablespoons flour* |
| | *Chopped fennel and parsley* |
| | *2 handfuls of baked breadcrumbs* |
| | *Pepper* |

Boil and mash potatoes. Put the fish in a saucepan and add 1 pint (550 ml) of the milk. Bring to the boil, remove from heat, and leave with the lid on until cool. Strain, keeping the milk. Flake the fish.

Make a cheese sauce by melting the butter in a saucepan, add flour off the heat. Mix well and slowly add fish milk, then the extra ½ pint. Add cheese, cook until melted. Season well with pepper. Check salt because the haddock may already be salty.

Mix the sauce with the fish and mashed potatoes, parsley, fennel and potted shrimps. Put in a buttered fireproof dish and sprinkle with breadcrumbs.*

Bake for ¾ hour in hot oven, 425°F 220°C gas 7. Sprinkle with chopped parsley and serve.

PREPARATION TIME 30 minutes COOKING TIME 45 minutes.

*This can be assembled the day before and left in the refrigerator covered with cling film.

## GREEN SALAD WITH HOT BUTTER DRESSING

| | |
|---|---|
| 100 g | *4 oz butter* |
| | *2 good heads of lettuce* |
| | *Lemon* |
| | *Garlic* |
| | *Salt* |
| | *A pinch of sugar* |

This is quite delicious. I use two different sorts of lettuce if I have them in the garden.

Wash and dry the lettuce and arrange it in a salad bowl. Season lightly with salt and a pinch of sugar. At the last moment warm the butter into which you have pounded a very small piece of garlic and a squeeze (literally) of lemon juice. Toss the lettuce in this.

If I can get a Cambozala cheese I serve this, or local Cheddar, afterwards with good bread.

# Saturday Lunch

(for 6 people)

## CRUDITES WITH MAYONNAISE

225 g    *8 oz button mushrooms*
        *1 head of celery*
450 g    *1 lb carrots*
        *Radishes*
        *1 cauliflower*
        *2 bunches spring onions*

MAYONNAISE

        *3 egg yolks*
425 ml    *¾ pint olive oil*
        *Squeeze of lemon juice*
        *Seasoning*

Make the mayonnaise (see page 116). If you wish you can have two bowls of varying flavours by adding curry powder to one or garlic to another. These can be made in advance and left covered in a cool place. I find mine sometimes curdles if left in the fridge so I leave it on top.

Most of the vegetables can be prepared the day before. Put the celery into iced water a few hours before serving to crisp it up. If the carrots are new from your garden pull them as near the time of eating as possible so they do not lose their flavour.

Slice the mushrooms. Trim the radishes and onions. Break the cauliflower into sprigs. Leave the carrots whole if they are young, or cut into long slices if old. Cut up celery.

Arrange all the prepared vegetables around a dish in heaps, with mayonnaises separately.

## CHEESE TART

PASTRY

225 g    *8 oz plain flour*
50 g    *2 oz butter (cold)*
50 g    *2 oz lard (cold)*
        *3–4 tablespoons iced water*
        *Pinch of salt*

FILLING

275 ml    *½ pint double cream*
150 g    *6 oz Cheddar, grated*
        *3 beaten eggs*
        *Salt and pepper*
        *Nutmeg*

VINAIGRETTE

        *4 tablespoons olive oil*
        *1 tablespoon wine vinegar*
        *1 dessertspoon any French*
          *mustard*
        *Black pepper and salt*

Make the pastry. Chill for ½ hour.* Line a 9-inch (22-cm) flan dish and bake blind for 10 minutes in hot oven, 400°F 200°C gas 6.

Mix the cream, cheese and eggs together. Season. Pour into previously cooked flan case and cook in preheated oven, 400–450°F 200–220°C gas 6–7, for about ½ hour or until golden brown and slightly risen.

*The pastry case can be made the day before, uncooked. Put filling in just before cooking.

Serve with a plain green salad and vinaigrette.

# Saturday Dinner

## (for 8 people)

### STUFFED TOMATOES

*16 good-sized tomatoes*
*4 large Boursin garlic*
  *cheeses*
*2 sticks celery, chopped*
  *finely or*
*1 heaped tablespoon chopped*
  *green pepper or cucumber*
*Salt and pepper*
*1 large bunch watercress*
*French dressing*

Skin the tomatoes, cut a slice off each one, scoop out seeds and core very carefully. Turn upside down and leave to drain. Mash the cheese and add the celery or greenpepper or cucumber. Stuff or pipe into the prepared tomatoes. Chill and serve on a dish with watercress bunches which have been dipped in French dressing. Hand brown bread and butter slices.

The tomatoes can be prepared the day before, but do not fill the tomatoes too far in advance or the filling will become soggy.

### FILLET OF BEEF WITH A WINE BUTTER

2 kg *4 lb (or 2 × 2 lb) fillet*
  *of beef*

**WINE BUTTER**

150 ml *¼ pint red wine*
*1 tablespoon finely*
  *chopped shallot*
175 g *6 oz softened butter*
*1 tablespoon lemon juice*
*1 tablespoon finely*
  *chopped parsley*

You can use left-over wine for this recipe but it should not be too old and vinegary!

Reduce the wine and shallots in a small saucepan over a high heat to about 5–6 tablespoons. Pour into a mixing bowl and while still warm but *not* hot whisk hard with the other ingredients. (This can be done in a Magimix.)* Serve semi-soft, not chilled.

Preheat the oven to 400–450°F 200°C gas 6. Brush the beef with olive oil and cook for 20 minutes, basting every 10.

PREPARATION TIME 10 minutes.

*Can be made a day in advance.

**FRIED POTATO CAKE**

*8 medium-sized potatoes*
*2 cloves of garlic, crushed*
*2 tablespoons butter*
*2 tablespoons oil*

Bake the potatoes in their skins for 1 hour. Remove skins and break up and mix in the garlic. Melt the butter and oil in a large frying pan, add the potato mixture and flatten it down and fry until the bottom is golden. Turn over and keep flattening it out. Turn out on to a dish and fold over like a pancake. Will keep in warmer.

**COURGETTES FRIED**
**IN BUTTER AND PARSLEY**

*1 medium courgette per*
  *person*
*2 tablespoons parsley*
*Butter*

Cut the courgettes into ½-inch (1-cm) slices and fry in butter and parsley till golden.

Follow with a fruit salad of grapes, melon and greengages.

# Sunday Lunch

(for 6 people)

## ARTICHOKES

6 artichokes trimmed at the bottom and boiled for about 40 minutes or until bottom leaves come away.

Serve with either cold vinaigrette as for Saturday lunch if the day is hot, or 8 oz (225 g) of melted butter if cold.

## CHICKEN WITH ALMOND SAUCE

| | |
|---|---|
| 2–2½ kg | *4–5 lb chicken* |
| 50 g | *2 oz butter* |
| | *A sprig of tarragon* |
| 425 ml | *¾ pint chicken stock* |
| 50 g | *2 oz blanched almonds* |
| 12 g | *½ oz flour* |
| | *Salt* |
| | *A pinch of sugar* |
| | *Ground mace* |
| | *2 tablespoons cream* |
| | *3 red peppers sliced and sautéed in butter* |

Put the tarragon and ½ oz (12 g) of the butter inside the chicken, rub another ounce of butter over the bird, cover with foil, put in a roasting tin and surround with ½ pint (275 ml) of stock. Roast for 20 minutes per pound (450 g) and 20 minutes over. After half an hour remove foil.

Meanwhile chop the almonds as finely as possible, put in frying pan with the remaining butter and cook slowly until pale golden brown. Blend in the flour, add chicken stock, season with salt, sugar and mace, simmer for 5 minutes.

Carve the bird, arrange on a serving dish, add the cream to the sauce and spoon over. Garnish with peppers.

## NEW POTATOES COOKED IN BUTTER AND BREADCRUMBS

| | |
|---|---|
| 1 kg | *Enough small new potatoes for six people* |
| | *2 good tablespoons butter* |
| | *2 tablespoons white breadcrumbs* |

This is the most delicious way to cook new potatoes.

If the potatoes are large, slice them thickly. Choose a thick pan in which the potatoes will fit all in one layer. Put in the butter, cover and cook over a very gentle heat for about 40 minutes – the butter must not burn. Take the potatoes out of the pan and arrange in an oven-proof dish. Sprinkle on the breadcrumbs and pour over the melted butter from the pan so that the breadcrumbs absorb the butter. Put in a hot oven, 450°F 230°C gas 8, for about 10 minutes.

The potatoes can be cooked in butter in advance and just kept warm, with the breadcrumbs added just before serving.

## BLACKCURRANT FOOL

| | |
|---|---|
| 1 kg | *2 lb blackcurrants, fresh or frozen* |
| | *4 tablespoons sugar* |
| | *Juice of ½ lemon* |
| 275 ml | *½ pint cream* |

This should be made one hour before the meal.

Stew the blackcurrants, stems and all, in a little water until soft (about 10 minutes), sieve. Sweeten to taste and add lemon juice. Serve while still warm. Pass whipped cream separately.

# Sally Wigram

*Friday*

**SUPPER**

Moussaka
Crunchy Webb Lettuce Salad

Fruit and Cheese

*Saturday*

**LUNCH**

Chicken Liver Pâté

Cold Ham and Salami
French Bread
Green Salad

**DINNER**

Watercress Soup

Baked Trout with Hollandaise Sauce
French Beans

Peach and Redcurrant Fruit Salad

*Sunday*

**LUNCH**

Barbecued Chicken and Sausages
New Potatoes
Mixed Salad

Cornetto Ice Cream

**SUPPER**

Eggs

# Friday Supper
## (for 6 people)

### MOUSSAKA

| | |
|---|---|
| 1 kg | *2 lb minced beef* |
| | *1 large onion, chopped* |
| | *1 clove garlic, crushed* |
| | *1 tablespoon tomato purée* |
| | *1 bay leaf* |
| | *1 tin artichoke hearts* |
| | *or* |
| 350 g | *¾ lb mushrooms* |
| | *1 beef stock cube* |
| | *Dash of Worcester sauce* |
| | *8 drops of Tabasco* |
| 150 ml | *¼ pint tomato juice* |
| | *Salt and pepper* |
| 25 g | *1 oz margarine or butter* |
| | *1 tablespoon oil* |
| | *1 dessertspoon flour* |
| | |
| | **SAUCE** |
| 50 g | *2 oz margarine or butter* |
| 50 g | *2 oz flour* |
| 275–425 ml | *½–¾ pint milk* |
| 75 g | *3 oz Cheddar* |
| | *Salt and pepper* |

Melt the margarine or butter and oil in a large saucepan. Add the garlic and onion and sauté until soft and transparent. Add the mince, stir in the flour and cook for 2–3 minutes. Pour on the tomato juice and crumbled stock cube, Worcester sauce, Tabasco, salt, pepper and bay leaf. Simmer for a further 5 minutes.

Meanwhile, place either the artichoke hearts (well drained and cut in four) or the sautéed mushrooms in the bottom of a gratin dish. Pour over the mince and dot with tomato purée.

TO MAKE THE SAUCE melt the margarine or butter in a saucepan, add the flour off the heat and stir in the milk until thick and smooth. Add two thirds of the grated cheese and cook. Pour the sauce over the mince when the mince is cool. Sprinkle the remaining cheese on top.* Put in a moderate oven, 375°F 190°C gas 5, for ½ hour, and just before serving brown under the grill.

PREPARATION TIME 40 minutes.

*All of this can be prepared in advance.

# Saturday Lunch

### CHICKEN LIVER PATE

| | |
|---|---|
| 225 g | *8 oz chicken livers* |
| | *2 hard-boiled eggs* |
| | *1 onion, chopped* |
| | *1 clove of garlic, chopped* |
| | *½ glass of left-over red wine* |
| | *Salt and pepper* |
| | *Knob of butter or* |
| | *margarine* |

Melt the butter in a frying pan and fry the onion and garlic. Roll the chicken livers in flour and sauté them together with onions and garlic until cooked – about 6 minutes. Chop up the chicken livers until fine, add the chopped eggs, and with a fork mash it well together, adding salt, black pepper and the red wine. Squash this mixture into any small pâté dish and eat it with hot toast or French bread.

Those who do not want to eat bread can eat this pâté with cold ham and salami and a large bowl of green salad.

# Saturday Dinner

(for 8 people)

## WATERCRESS SOUP

*2 large potatoes*
*1 large onion*
*2 bunches watercress*
*Tabasco*
*1 chicken stock cube*
850 ml *1½ pints milk*
*2 tablespoons cream*
*Salt*

This can be eaten either cold or hot depending on the weather.

Peel the onions and potatoes and twist the stalks off the watercress. Put them all in a saucepan and just cover with water. Add a stock cube, 3 dashes of Tabasco and a pinch of salt. Bring to the boil and simmer for 15 minutes. Blend in a liquidizer with ½ pint of milk, then add the rest of the milk. Reheat or chill. Stir in the cream before serving.

PREPARATION TIME 20 minutes.

## BAKED TROUT WITH HOLLANDAISE SAUCE

2 × 1 kg *2 brown trout weighing about 2 lb each*
*Oil and butter*
*Juice of 1 lemon*
*Salt and pepper*

HOLLANDAISE SAUCE

*2 egg yolks*
350 g *12 oz butter*
*Juice of 1 lemon*
*Salt and pepper*
*Chopped chives*

Put a large piece of foil on a baking sheet and oil it well. Place the fish on the foil, rub butter on to their skins and sprinkle salt and pepper over them. Squeeze the lemon juice over them and wrap them up carefully. Bake in a medium oven, 350°F 180°C gas 4, for ½ hour. (I usually peel some skin off the tail end to see if they are cooked.)

The essential part of hollandaise making is the arm-breaking whisking. Without this the sauce will never be light and frothy. In a double saucepan heat the egg yolks, lemon juice and a large knob of butter. Divide the rest of the butter into 7 or 8 small pieces. As the mixture in the pan melts together, start to beat well with a wire whisk, adding the pieces of butter one at a time. The sauce thickens with the beating and when it begins to thicken *then* add the butter. If it becomes too thick at the end you can add a spoonful of boiling water (this is also supposed to halt curdling).

Serve the trout, skinned, on a large plate, with the hollandaise in a sauce bowl, adding the chives just before serving.

Serve with French beans, boiled in salted water for 4 minutes.

## PEACH AND REDCURRANT FRUIT SALAD

*8 peaches*
250–500 g *1–2 punnets of redcurrants*
*Juice of 1 lemon*
*A little white sugar*

This has a good tart taste after the richness of the trout and hollandaise.

Peel the peaches, slice them into a serving bowl and cover with the topped and tailed redcurrants. Squeeze the lemon over the top and sprinkle with a little white sugar.

# Sunday Lunch

(for 6 people)

---

## BARBECUED CHICKEN AND SAUSAGES

*12 sausages*
*12 chicken pieces*

This is cooked outside on a barbecue which my husband is in charge of. The ketchup in the marinade may sound disgusting, but it does make the chicken taste good.

MARINADE

150 ml  *¼ pint oil*
*2 tablespoons tomato
  ketchup*
*2 tablespoons white wine*
*Salt and pepper*

Marinade the chicken in the oil, ketchup, white wine and seasoning for about 2 hours.

Serve with new potatoes and a mixed salad.

No pudding has ever been as popular as *Cornetto Ice Creams*.

# Sunday Supper

Scrambled eggs in London

---

# SEPTEMBER

## Sally Worthington

*Sally Worthington's house is over three
hundred years old. Rambling and timber-framed,
it was originally a farmhouse.*

*Friday*

**SUPPER**

Tuna and Bean Salad

Spinach and Curd Cheese Pancakes

*Saturday*

**LUNCH**

Veal and Ham Pie
Green Salad and Blue Cheese Dressing
Baked Potatoes

Caramel Ice Cream with Walnuts

**DINNER**

Fish Pâté and Green Mayonnaise

Lamb with Coriander and Mushrooms
Potato Gratin
Runner Beans

Almond Cheese Sablées

*Sunday*

**LUNCH**

Roast Gammon with Spiced Pears
Boiled Potatoes
Green Peas and Lettuce

Special Blackberry and Apple Summer Pudding

**SUPPER**

Tomato Goo and Welsh Rarebits
Gammon and eggs *sur le plat*

# *Friday Supper*

## (for 6 people)

### TUNA AND BEAN SALAD

| | |
|---|---|
| 2 × 425 g | 2 × 15 oz tins red kidney beans |
| 250 g | 7 oz tin of tuna fish |
| | 2 tablespoons chopped |
| | spring onions (include some |
| | of the green tops) |
| | 1 tablespoon chopped |
| | parsley |
| | 6 tablespoons olive oil |
| | 1 tablespoon lemon juice |
| | Salt and pepper |
| | French mustard |
| | Sugar |

Make a vinaigrette by whisking together the oil, lemon, salt, pepper, mustard and sugar. Mix the spring onions, tuna fish and beans together carefully, toss them in the salad dressing and sprinkle with chopped parsley.

### SPINACH AND CURD CHEESE PANCAKES

PANCAKE BATTER

| | |
|---|---|
| | 6 tablespoons flour |
| | ½ teaspoon salt |
| | 3 eggs |
| 425 ml | ¾ pint milk |

FILLING

| | |
|---|---|
| 500 g | 1 large packet frozen or |
| | 1 lb fresh spinach |
| 175 g | 6 oz curd cheese or cream |
| | cheese |
| | Lots of salt and freshly |
| | ground black pepper |

CHEESE SAUCE

| | |
|---|---|
| 425 ml | ¾ pint milk |
| | 1 heaped tablespoon butter |
| | 1 heaped tablespoon flour |
| 50 g | 2 oz Cheddar or Gruyère |
| | Salt and pepper |
| | 1 teaspoon English mustard |

To make the pancake batter, sieve the flour and salt together in a bowl, make a well in the centre, break the eggs into the well, add a small quantity of milk and mix this into the eggs. With a wooden spoon gradually incorporate the flour into the egg and milk. As more flour is drawn in add the extra liquid. (Alternatively make the batter in a food mixer.) Let it stand for a couple of hours if possible.

For each pancake: heat 1 teaspoon of oil or a little clarified butter in a small frying pan until smoking, then turn the heat down a little. Put in 2 tablespoons of batter, swirling the pan to allow it to cover the entire surface thinly. Cook on one side only until bottom is golden brown. Lift out and put on plate. Repeat until all the mixture is used up.*

Cook the spinach in butter until soft (about 10 minutes). If frozen drain very well. Chop roughly and mix with the curd cheese. I put mine altogether in a Magimix.* Season very well and put a scant tablespoon of the mixture in to each pancake. Roll up and put in a well buttered ovenproof dish.

Make the cheese sauce: melt the butter in a saucepan, add the flour off the heat, return to heat and add the milk slowly. Add the cheese and cook for a few minutes. Season to taste, adding mustard.*

Pour the sauce over the pancakes and glaze under grill or in a hot oven.

Serve with a green salad.

*The pancakes, spinach filling and cheese sauce can be made the day before and kept in separate bowls covered in cling film. Pancakes freeze very well.

# Saturday Lunch

(for 6 people)

### VEAL AND HAM PIE

**SHORTCRUST PASTRY**

225 g  *8 oz flour*
40 g  *1½ oz lard*
65 g  *2½ oz butter*
*4 tablespoons ice cold water*
*Salt*
*1 egg yolk*

**FILLING**

1 kg  *2 lb veal  thinly sliced
and  eaten*
225 kg  *8 oz cu  d ham*
225 kg  *8 oz streaky bacon, with
rinds removed*
*6 hard-boiled eggs, quartered*
225 kg  *8 oz mushrooms, sliced*
300 g  *1 tin consommé*
*2 tablespoons mixed herbs*
*Mace*

Make the pastry and leave in fridge for ½ hour.

Cut the veal into oblongs about 2 inches by 3 inches (5 cm by 8 cm). Season each piece with mace, salt and pepper and plenty of chopped herbs. Lay a piece of bacon (cut to the same size as the veal) on top and roll up. Arrange the rolls in a buttered pie dish, interspersing with cubed ham, mushrooms and hard-boiled eggs. Sprinkle with the rest of the herbs and pour in consommé.

Cover with pastry, decorate and brush with an egg yolk which has been beaten with a pinch of salt.* Bake in a medium oven, 350°F 180°C gas 4, for 1½ hours.

Serve cold.

*The pie can be made on Thursday and cooked on Friday.

**GREEN SALAD WITH BLUE
CHEESE DRESSING**

50 g  *2 oz Stilton*
275 ml  *½ pint mayonnaise*
*2 tablespoons double cream*
*1 tablespoon chopped parsley
and sage*
*1 clove of garlic, crushed*
*Salt and pepper*
*1 large Webbs or Cos lettuce*

Make the mayonnaise (see page 116). Crumble or finely dice the cheese, stir in the mayonnaise. Put into a Magimix or liquidizer with the herbs, garlic, salt and pepper. Blend. Pour over the salad at the last moment.

Serve with baked potatoes (1 per person). Rub with olive oil and salt, prick with a fork and bake in a hot oven for approximately one hour.

### CARAMEL ICE CREAM WITH WALNUTS

4 tablespoons sugar
2 egg yolks
275 ml ½ pint double cream, whipped
Chopped walnuts
Maple syrup

This must be made at least the day before. It unfreezes very quickly so take it out of the deep freeze just before serving.

Put the sugar in a saucepan with about 2 tablespoons of water, stir over a low heat until the sugar has dissolved, then boil until light brown. Pour in 4 more tablespoons of water and simmer, stirring until it is thoroughly mixed in. Beat the egg yolks, pour the syrup on to them slowly, and stir until the mixture thickens (use an electric hand whisk if possible). Fold in the cream, put into box and freeze until solid. Serve in individual glass bowls garnished with chopped walnuts and about a tablespoon of maple syrup per bowl.

# Saturday Dinner

## (for 8 people)

### FISH PATE

| | |
|---|---|
| 500 g | *1 lb filleted cod, haddock or any other white fish* |
| | *2 eggs* |
| 75 g | *3 oz white breadcrumbs* |
| 275 ml | *½ pint double cream* |
| 1 kg | *2 handfuls sorrel or spinach* |
| | *1 handful parsley* |
| | *1 bunch spring onions* |
| 50 g | *2 oz butter* |
| | *Salt and freshly ground black pepper* |

This should be made a day in advance.

Purée the fish with the eggs, breadcrumbs and cream. Season well. Bring a large pan of water to the boil, add the parsley and sorrel (or spinach) and spring onions. Cook for about 5 minutes, until tender. Drain very well, add the butter and purée.

Put half the fish mixture into a well buttered loaf tin, cover with three quarters of the spinach purée (keep the rest for the green mayonnaise), then add the rest of the fish. Cover with foil and cook in a *bain marie* at 350°F 180°C gas 4 for ¾ hour. Chill overnight. Turn out on to serving dish and decorate with fresh tarragon or dill. Serve with a green mayonnaise.

### GREEN MAYONNAISE

| | |
|---|---|
| | *1–2 tablespoons white wine or vermouth* |
| | *2 egg yolks* |
| 275 ml | *½ pint olive oil* |
| | *Salt and pepper* |
| | *1 teaspoon white wine vinegar* |
| | *1 teaspoon French mustard* |

This can be flavoured either with the same spinach or sorrel and parsley purée, or a mixture of other green herbs such as chervil, chives and marjoram or, as it is for fish, dill.

Put the egg yolks and mustard into a bowl and whisk, slowly adding the olive oil. Add the vinegar and season well.*

Thin with white wine or vermouth and mix in the spinach purée.

*Can be made a day in advance.

### LAMB WITH CORIANDER AND MUSHROOMS

| | |
|---|---|
| 1¾ kg | *4 lb boned leg of lamb* |
| | *1 tablespoon coriander seed, crushed* |
| | *1 clove garlic* |
| 350 g | *12 oz mushrooms* |
| | *1 rounded tablespoon chopped parsley* |
| | *Salt and freshly ground black pepper* |
| | *1 tablespoon butter* |

Crush the garlic, mix with the crushed coriander seeds and spread over the cut surface of the meat, season with salt and pepper. Cut the mushrooms into quarters and sauté in butter for a few minutes. Mix with the chopped parsley. Put the mixture into the bone space of the lamb and sew up. Put into roasting pan with some good dripping and roast for 1½ hours at 400°F 200°C gas 6.

# Saturday Dinner

continued

---

### POTATO GRATIN

750 g   *1½ lb potatoes (new if possible)*
425 ml   *¾ pint milk*
275 ml   *½ pint cream*
        *6 tablespoons grated*
          *Gruyère*
        *2 tablespoons freshly*
          *grated Parmesan*
        *Butter*
        *Salt and freshly ground*
          *black pepper*

Peel and slice the potatoes and put in an ovenproof dish, cover with milk and season. Cook in a hot oven for about 20 minutes or until half done. Drain, add the cream and sprinkle with the cheeses; dot with butter and cook in a moderate oven, 350°F 180°C gas 4, for 30 minutes (cover with foil if the top gets too brown).

Serve with runner beans, sliced and plunged into boiling salted water for about 7 minutes. They should still be firm.

### ALMOND CHEESE SABLEES

### BISCUITS

175 g   *6 oz plain flour*
125 g   *4 oz butter*
35 g   *1½ oz ground almonds*
75 g   *3 oz strong Cheddar, grated*
       *Plenty of paprika*
       *Salt and pepper*
       *2 egg yolks*

### FILLING

       *1 egg white*
       *1 teaspoon cornflour*
       *1 egg yolk*
       *1 teaspoon paprika*
35 g   *1½ oz Cheddar, grated*
150 ml   *¼ pint warm milk*
       *Salt and pepper*

Rub the flour and butter together until the mixture looks like breadcrumbs. Add the ground almonds, Cheddar, paprika, salt and pepper. Beat 1 egg yolk with ½ teaspoon of water and mix with the dry ingredients (add more water only if necessary).

Roll out thinly and cut into little 1 or 2-inch (2 or 4-cm) rounds. Brush with a beaten egg yolk. Bake at 350°F 180°C gas 4, for about 20 minutes or until golden. Cool on rack.

This pastry can be made in advance and frozen; or the biscuits, once cooked, will keep in a tin for a few days.

Mix the cornflour with the egg and paprika. Season. Put in a saucepan and gradually mix in the cheese. Warm the milk and mix in. Continue stirring and bring to the boil. Take off heat.*

Whip the egg white very stiffly and fold into the mixture. Return to the heat and cook for a minute or two more, stirring with a folding motion.

TO SERVE Reheat the biscuits in a moderate oven for about 15 minutes and either make them into sandwiches or put a dollop of filling on top of each.

*Can be made in advance.

### ROAST GAMMON

| | |
|---|---|
| 2¾ kg | 6 lb gammon joint soaked overnight in cold water |
| | 1 tablespoon brown sugar |
| | Bay leaf |
| | Peppercorns |

**GLAZE**

| | |
|---|---|
| 175 g | 6 oz brown sugar |
| | Juice of ½ lemon |
| | 3 tablespoons water |
| | 2 tablespoons made-up English mustard |

**SPICED PEARS**

| | |
|---|---|
| 1¾ kg | 4 lb cooking pears |
| 575 ml | 1 pint white malt vinegar |
| 1 kg | 2 lb sugar |
| | 8 cloves |
| | 4 teaspoons allspice berries |
| 50 g | 2 oz cinnamon sticks |
| | Squeeze of lemon juice |

**GREEN PEAS AND LETTUCE**

| | |
|---|---|
| 2 × 250 g | 2 packets frozen petit pois |
| | 1 lettuce |
| | 2 bunches spring onions |
| 150 ml | ¼ pint water |
| | 1 tablespoon castor sugar |
| 65 g | 2½ oz butter |
| | 1 teaspoon flour |
| | Salt |
| | Freshly ground black pepper |

This is good hot or cold but I prefer it hot.

Put the gammon in a large saucepan, cover with water and add brown sugar, bay leaf and peppercorns. Bring to the boil very gently, turn down heat and simmer for half the cooking time, which should be calculated at 20 minutes to the lb (450 g) and 20 minutes over.

Combine the brown sugar, lemon juice, water and mustard together and cook gently until sugar is dissolved, then boil to a thin syrup. When the gammon is half cooked remove it from the water and take off the skin. Score the fat into diamonds with a knife, pour over the glaze and cook in a medium oven, 350°F 180°C gas 4, for the rest of the cooking time, basting repeatedly with the glaze.

Peel, core and quarter the pears, put into water and lemon juice to cover. Put the rest of the ingredients into a saucepan and stir over a gentle heat to dissolve the sugar. Add the pears and bring to the boil. Reduce the heat and cook until tender over a simmering heat. Pack into jars.*

*This can all be done days in advance.

Serve with plain boiled potatoes, sprinkled with parsley.

Shred the lettuce. Halve the spring onions if large. Put the peas in a saucepan with the lettuce, spring onions, castor sugar, 2 oz (50 g) of butter, salt and pepper. Cover with the water and bring gently to the boil, shaking the pan occasionally. Cream ½ oz (15 g) butter with the flour and stir into mixture off the heat.* Reheat until mixture thickens slightly.

*This can be made the day before.

# *Sunday Lunch*

continued

### BLACKBERRY SUMMER PUDDING

This must be made a day in advance. It freezes very well.

¾–1 kg  *1½–2 lb blackberries*
  *2 apples, peeled, cored and sliced*
50 g  *2 oz sugar*
275 ml  *½ pint water*
  *½ thin sliced white loaf*
  *A little cornflour*

Put the water in a saucepan with the sugar, dissolve and boil rapidly for 5 minutes. Add the fruit and simmer until soft. Strain, keeping juice. Put through a Mouli or sieve and add half of the juice. Test for sweetness.

Cover the bottom of an ovenproof glass soufflé dish with de-crusted bread cut to shape. Cover with a good layer of purée, and continue layering until you reach the top of the bowl, checking that each layer is well covered with fruit. Put a plate on top and leave overnight or longer.

Thicken the rest of the juice with a little cornflour, and when turning out the pudding pour over a little of this sauce; otherwise hand it separately. Serve with thick cream, either separately or smothered, not piped, over the top.

PREPARATION TIME 20 minutes.

# Sunday Supper

## (for 2 people)

### TOMATO GOO

*5 cooking tomatoes (or some from my deep freeze)*
*Olive oil*
*Large handful of mint or basil*
*Salt and pepper*
*Sugar*
150 ml  *¼ pint cream*

Skin the tomatoes and cook in a large saucepan with olive oil, mint, salt, pepper and plenty of sugar. Cook until thick. Reduce a little. Just before serving stir in cream, heat through and check the seasoning.

Serve with Welsh Rarebit to mop up the remains.

### WELSH RAREBIT

*4 slices white bread*
*English mustard*
150 g  *About 6 oz strong Cheddar, grated*
*Worcester sauce*

Spread the bread very thinly with English mustard. Cover thickly with grated cheese. (I sometimes add a little Stilton.) Add a good shake of Worcester sauce to each slice and put under hot grill until melted. Cut into quarters and pile up on plate.
   Must be eaten immediately.

### GAMMON AND EGGS

Put slices of cold gammon from lunch into greased individual fire-proof dishes. Break in two eggs per dish. Season well and cook in a hot oven until whites are just set – about 7 minutes.

## FLAPJACKS

150 g   *5 oz butter*
150 g   *5 oz brown sugar*
150 g   *5 oz Scott's porage oats*

Melt the butter and sugar together, add the oats and mix together well. Spread on to a greased shallow baking tin about 7 inches × 11 inches (18-cm × 28-cm) and bake at 350°F 180°C gas 4 for 15–20 minutes. (Make sure they don't burn.) Take out and mark into bars when set, but not cold. Ease out and cool on a rack.

## CHOCOLATE CAKE

225 g   *8 oz dark chocolate*
225 g   *8 oz butter*
275 g   *10 oz dark brown sugar*
125 g   *4 oz fresh white breadcrumbs*
125 g   *4 oz ground almonds*
        *6 egg yolks*
        *6 egg whites, stiffly beaten*

### FILLING

75 g   *3 oz icing sugar*
25 g   *1 oz cocoa powder*
35 g   *1½ oz butter*
50 g   *2 oz castor sugar*
       *or*
       *Apricot jam or whipped
         cream*

This is a delicious rich cake which keeps well for several days.

You will need 3 7-inch (18-cm) sandwich tins, lined with greaseproof paper, buttered and dusted with flour. Preheat the oven to 375°F 190°C gas 5. Melt the chocolate with 11 tablespoons of water in a double saucepan. Cool. Beat the butter and the sugar together until soft, then add the egg yolks, almonds and breadcrumbs. Mix in the melted chocolate and fold in the egg whites. Put into the cake tins and place in the oven for 40 minutes. Take out and leave to cool in their tins and then turn out on to a rack.

Sift the icing sugar and cocoa into a bowl. Put the butter with 2 tablespoons of water and the castor sugar into a saucepan and just bring to the boil, then add to the sugar and cocoa. Mix well. When cool use to sandwich the cake.

# Children's Food

I always have food in the deep freeze for the children, especially useful when I have a dinner party or for some reason we are going to eat a very late lunch.

LASAGNE (see page 48).

PANCAKES (see page 153). For the children I usually stuff these with mince cooked with tomatoes, herbs, onions and covered in a cheese sauce. Alternatively, diced cooked chicken, sweetcorn and a few peas for colour, again covered in a white sauce.

SAUSAGE ROLLS Make one huge roll with an 8 oz (225 g) packet of frozen puff pastry rolled out into an oblong. Place 1 lb ($\frac{1}{2}$ kg) minced belly pork, seasoned with rosemary, salt and pepper and a chopped onion, down the centre. Cut slits in the long sides and cross over each other (rather like a plait), pulling firmly in and wetting the joints. Alternatively, make individual rolls – roll out the pastry and cut into strips, add filling, roll up and slash the top of each. Glaze with beaten egg and sprinkle with sea salt. Bake in a hot oven, 400°F 200°C gas 6, until well risen, about 15 minutes.

PIZZAS I keep two or three pizzas in the deep freeze and add special toppings for the children: grated mozzarella or Cheddar, diced ham or sliced salami (see page 167).

CHILDREN'S PUDDINGS

ICE CREAM home-made (see page 130)

MERINGUES (see page 97)

BANANAS AND CREAM PUDDING Slice 1 banana per person into a pie dish, cover with a hot sugar syrup and when cold cover with whipped cream and grated chocolate.

# Rosamund Wallinger

great many of Rosamund's weekends are spent in France. She rents a beautiful little French farmhouse in the Calvados country, surrounded by ancient apples trees, a few sheep and some cows.

Rosamund, who used to be a professional cook, finds shopping in France a pleasure rather than a chore. 'There is a market,' she says, 'in each town once a week. Having two towns nearby, I go marketing twice weekly. I buy fruit and vegetables, and although the quality is no better than in England there is a much wider variety. I take with me a large jar which is then filled with thick cream scooped out of a bucket. The butter is also sold from a tub.

'I would never buy any pre-packed goods, like cheeses. The market sells rounds of Camembert and a vast selection of local cheeses, all of them fresh from the local farms, and it's quite possible to stop at any little farm and buy direct. The price happily is standardized. Some of these farms also sell Calvados which they have made; it's quite delicious, though if you buy an *hors d'age* you can pay as much as sixteen pounds a bottle.'

There is a daily trip to the *boulangerie* to get hot croissants for breakfast and bread for lunch. 'I occasionally buy a *pâtisserie*,' says Rosamund, 'for a picnic or a special occasion – strawberry tarts are wonderful but they are very expensive.

'Supermarket shopping in France is also more enjoyable, compared with England; everything is much more personal. At the meat department, for instance, there is a butcher behind the counter who cuts the joints individually – and who expects a tip for reserving the best for you. The staff never seem to change and the whole atmosphere is more friendly. I also buy wines there – excellent *vin ordinaire* – for about sixty pence a bottle.'

The white wines Rosamund drinks almost exclusively are: 1976 Meursault Lupe Cholet and 1975 Chassagne-Montrachet, both white Burgundies, lovely, but expensive. Sauvignon, which is a good and cheaper white wine, she likes especially with spicy food or mixed with Cassis. The clarets she drinks are: 1970 Château Giscours, 1970 Château Gruaud – Larose, 1975 Château Cos – Labory and 1975 Château Beaumont de Bolivar – all expensive and still rather young – or 1970 Château Maine Gazin or 1970 Château Cap St Martin.

Because it is a holiday home, everything is very relaxed and informal. 'I love cooking, but my recipes for weekends are always simple. I think it is risky to use one particular style of cooking for a series of meals; people may be bored by the same type of food, for instance French, or very rich, or vegetarian, so I aim for several courses as varied as possible, with a few unusual things that I hope people will remember and find impressive. I never serve large helpings – it's always better if you wish you'd had just a little bit more.'

Rosamund's breakfasts are very French: hot croissants with cherry jam or marmalade, the delicious local butter and lots of coffee. Cereals are available for the Anglophil. Her kitchen is minuscule, with no gadgets whatsovever, save a spit in the oven (the French often bone their meat and then spit-roast it) and a coffee grinder. Just sharp knives and a balloon whisk. No deep-freeze or dishwasher. She follows the sensible French habit of keeping the same plate, knives and forks for the first two courses. Every meal is accompanied by wine, and in the evenings dinner is followed by a large glass of Calvados in front of a huge log fire.

*Friday*

**SUPPER**

Boned and Stuffed Country Chicken
Chicory, Lettuce and Apple Salad

Peaches in Brandy

*Saturday*

**LUNCH**

Big Top Pizza
French Bean Salad

Raspberry Ice Cream

**DINNER**

Crab Custards

Sweetbreads on Croûtons
Steamed Broccoli

Spicy French Apple Flan

*Sunday*

**LUNCH**

Roast Boned Shoulder of Lamb with Tarragon and Damson Jam
Roast Potatoes
Spinach Purée

Pineapple Brulée

**SUPPER**

Cheese Pudding
Celeriac and Carrot Salad

# Friday Supper

## (for 6 people)

### BONED AND STUFFED COUNTRY CHICKEN

| | |
|---|---|
| 2¼ kg | *1 large (5 lb) chicken* |
| 450 g | *1 lb sausagemeat* |
| | *1 level teaspoon allspice* |
| | *4 sage leaves, chopped* |
| | *2 tablespoons chopped* |
| | *parsley* |
| 50 g | *2 oz butter* |
| 450 g | *1 lb Cox's apples* |
| 50 g | *2 oz breadcrumbs* |
| | *1 egg, beaten* |
| | *8 tarragon leaves, chopped* |
| | *1 medium onion* |
| | *Salt and pepper* |

CHICORY, LETTUCE AND
APPLE SALAD

| | |
|---|---|
| 225 g | *8 oz chicory* |
| | *Crisp lettuce head* |
| 225 g | *8 oz dessert apples (unpeeled)* |
| | *Dressing* |

This should be made a day in advance.

Bone chicken (see page 47) or have your butcher bone it. Put carcase flat on a board.

Peel, core and finely chop apples. Mix together with sausagemeat, allspice, plenty of freshly ground salt and pepper, sage, tarragon, parsley, breadcrumbs and finely chopped onion. Bind together with the beaten egg and place in centre of chicken carcase. Pull sides up over stuffing and reshape vaguely like a chicken, then sew up the seams with yarn, remembering to close leg holes. Spread the outside of the chicken with the butter and wrap in foil.

Roast chicken in pre-heated oven, 375°F 190°C gas 5, for 1 hour 45 minutes, pull back foil to brown top for a further 15 minutes. Cool.

TO SERVE Slice like a loaf of bread.

Chop chicory; shred lettuce and chop apple. Mix together with a vinaigrette.

### HOT PEACHES IN BRANDY

| | |
|---|---|
| | *6 large peaches, skinned* |
| | *and sliced* |
| 50 g | *2 oz butter* |
| | *2 tablespoons brandy, or* |
| | *lemon juice* |
| 25 g | *1 oz castor sugar* |

Heat the butter and sugar gently in a frying pan until just turning brown.*

Add the peaches and cook for a further 2–3 minutes, stirring occasionally. Add the brandy and flame it, or add the lemon juice, and serve immediately.

*Can be prepared just before dinner.

# *Saturday Lunch*

## (for 6 people)

### BIG TOP PIZZA

DOUGH

225 g   *8 oz plain flour*
50 g   *2 oz butter*
35 ml   *½ gill milk*
  *1 teaspoon sugar*
  *½ teaspoon salt*
  *1 teaspoon dried yeast*
  *2 small eggs, beaten*

TOP

  *1 tablespoon olive oil*
  *2 teaspoons chopped basil*
225 g   *8 oz Mozzarella cheese*
450 g   *1 lb tomatoes*
  *1 small onion*
  *6–8 anchovy fillets*
  *Freshly ground salt and pepper*

FRENCH BEAN SALAD

1 kg   *2 lb pencil-thin French beans*
  *1 dessertspoon chopped dill*
  *Vinaigrette dressing*

Dissolve the sugar in the milk and warm this to blood temperature. Whisk in the dried yeast with a fork and leave to work for 10 minutes. Sift the flour and salt into a large bowl. Add the yeast and milk, the beaten eggs, soft butter and mix all together. Knead well. Cover and leave to rise in a warm place for about 40 minutes.

Shape the dough into a greased 9 or 10-inch (22 or 25-cm) flan ring.

Heat the olive oil in a frying pan. Add the thinly sliced onion, soften gently then add sliced tomatoes and cook gently for just half a minute. Remove from heat and add the herbs and seasoning. (If you cannot get basil add herbs according to taste, remembering that dried herbs are stronger than fresh.)

Cover the dough with the tomato mixture, place slices of cheese over that and finally add anchovy fillets cut into thin strips. You may now 'prove' the pizza for 10 minutes, but it is not strictly necessary.

Bake in pre-heated oven, 400°F 200°C gas 6, for about 30 minutes. Serve hot.

Wash the beans and steam them for 5 minutes. If you do not have a steamer plunge them into boiling salted water and cook for 6 minutes. Cool, cover and leave in the fridge until needed.

Make up salad dressing using olive oil, wine vinegar, freshly ground salt and pepper, castor sugar and the chopped dill. Pour over beans before serving.

### RASPBERRY ICE CREAM

If you grow September raspberries use these, but frozen summer ones will do as well.

1 kg   *2 lb raspberries*
175 g   *6 oz icing sugar*
425 ml   *¾ pint double cream*
  *Squeeze of lemon juice*

Sieve the raspberries to remove seeds. Beat the cream until thick but not stiff. Beat in the icing sugar, lemon juice and raspberry pulp. Pour this mixture into ice cream tray. Cover and freeze.

Three hours before serving remove from freezer. When the ice cream is a little softened beat or liquidize it, and return to freezer to re-harden.

Serve with chocolate Bath Olivers.

# Saturday Dinner

## (for 8 people)

### CRAB CUSTARDS

| | |
|---|---|
| 275 ml | *½ pint double cream* |
| 275 ml | *½ pint milk* |
| | *5 egg yolks* |
| | *3 egg whites* |
| 225 g | *8 oz crab meat (white and pink)* |
| | *2 bay leaves* |
| | *1 medium onion* |
| | *½ teaspoon grated nutmeg* |
| | *Salt and pepper* |

These are also very good flavoured with a strong cheese like Gruyère instead of crab.

Put the bay leaves and onion into the milk and bring slowly to the boil. Lightly beat the yolks and whites in a bowl. Add the cream to the hot milk and pour this over the eggs. Stir in the crab meat, then the grated nutmeg and seasoning.

Butter 8 ramekins and stand them in a shallow baking tin with water halfway up their sides. Pour the custard mixture carefully into the ramekins and bake in the centre of a slow oven, 325°F 170°C gas 3, for about 45 minutes or until custard is quite thick. Remove from oven and leave in a cool place – not the refrigerator, or they will lose flavour.*

Serve cold.

*Can be made a day in advance.

### SWEETBREADS ON CROUTONS

| | |
|---|---|
| 800 g | *1¾ lb calves' or lambs' sweetbreads* |
| | *1 medium onion* |
| 125 g | *4 oz butter* |
| | *6 slices white bread cut into 3-inch (8-cm) rounds* |
| | *1 tablespoon flour* |
| | *2 tablespoons brandy* |
| | *Salt and pepper* |
| | *½ tablespoon parsley, chopped* |

So many people think they dislike sweetbreads, but it is well worth trying this recipe: it is a rich and original dish.

Soak sweetbreads for 4 hours in cold water, changing it twice. Rinse them. Place in a pan of cold water, bring to the boil and simmer *very* gently for 9 minutes. Drain, cool, then remove all fat and skin. Trim to regular sizes.

Fry the croûtons in 2 oz (50 g) butter until golden on both sides.

Dust sweetbreads lightly with flour and sauté gently in 1½ oz (40 g) butter for about 8 minutes. Gently sweat the diced onion in ½ oz (12 g) butter for 3 minutes, then add to the sweetbreads. Season with freshly ground salt and pepper. Pile the sweetbread mixture on to croûtons and cook at 350°C 180°C gas 4 for 12 minutes.

When ready to serve pour a little brandy over the sweetbreads and decorate with fresh chopped parsley.

Serve with steamed broccoli.

### SPICY FRENCH APPLE FLAN

175 g  *6 oz flour*
25 g  *1 oz ground rice*
150 g  *5 oz butter*
*1 egg yolk*
50 g  *2 oz castor sugar*
*1 teaspoon cinnamon*
*1 teaspoon mixed spice*
1 kg  *2 lb cooking apples*
*Plum or damson jam for glaze*
*Juice and rind of ½ lemon*

Sift together the flour and ground rice. Cut in the butter and work with fingertips until mixture resembles breadcrumbs. Add the egg yolk, sugar and spices, and lightly knead together to make a dough. Rest pastry for 1 hour in cold place, then roll out fairly thickly and line a 7 or 8-inch (18 or 20-cm) flan ring.*

Peel, core and slice apples, then arrange over pastry. Squeeze over the lemon juice. Sprinkle on grated rind, then glaze with the warmed jam.

Bake in centre of pre-heated oven, 400°F 200°C gas 6, for about 45 minutes. If apples begin to brown too much cover with butter paper or foil for last few minutes. Serve warm.

*Can be prepared a day or two in advance and reheated.

# Sunday Lunch

## (for 6 people)

### ROAST BONED SHOULDER OF LAMB WITH TARRAGON AND DAMSON JAM

2¼ kg — 5 lb shoulder of lamb, boned but not rolled
3 tablespoons damson jam or redcurrant jelly
3 tablespoons chopped tarragon leaves

Fill the bone cavities and the underside of the joint with a layer of jam and tarragon leaves mixed together. Roll the shoulder with fatty layer outside, then taking a thin string and cooking needle sew it together into a Rugby ball shape. Spread a final layer of jam and tarragon over the surface, then enclose the joint in foil, leaving the top generously open to allow the meat to brown. Cook in a pre-heated oven, 350°F 180°C gas 4, for 2 hours 20 minutes (35 minutes to 1 lb – 450 g).

SPINACH PUREE

675 g — 1½ lb spinach

Wash spinach, steam for 6 minutes, cool slightly. Add salt and butter, then purée. Spinach can be reheated without losing its colour.

Serve with roast potatoes.

### PINEAPPLE BRULEE

This dish won a prize for me in the *Sunday Times* Best Cook in Britain Competition.

1 pineapple
275 ml — ½ pint double cream
4 dessertspoons castor sugar
3 tablespoons water

Place water and sugar in a non-stick saucepan and over very gentle heat dissolve sugar, without boiling. Then bring to rolling boil and cook until pale brown. Have a sheet of well-buttered greaseproof paper on a flat surface and pour the bubbling golden caramel all over surface. Leave to harden, then break into smallish pieces.
    Cut the pineapple into chunks and spread at the bottom of a glass bowl. Whip the cream until stiff and pile over the pineapple. Put in fridge until needed. At the last minute sprinkle the caramel pieces over the surface.

# Sunday Supper

(for 2 people)

### CHEESE PUDDING

225 g  *8 oz Gruyère or strong Cheddar*
75 g  *3 oz breadcrumbs·*
272 ml  *½ pint milk*
*5 eggs*
*1 teaspoon Worcester sauce*
*Salt and pepper*

This is as delicious as a soufflé but much easier to make, as only the whipped egg whites have to be added at the last minute; the rest can be made well in advance.

Grease an ovenproof soufflé dish. Mix together grated cheese, breadcrumbs, Worcester sauce, milk, seasoning and the yolks of the eggs and put into dish. Cover and leave until needed.

Whip egg whites stiffly and fold into mixture. Cook in pre-heated oven, 400°F 200°C gas 6, for about 30–40 minutes until well risen and brown on top.

Serve immediately.

### CELERIAC AND CARROT SALAD

*1 celeriac root*
*Juice of ½ lemon*
450 g  *1 lb carrots*
*Vinaigrette dressing*

The main course for this supper would be left-over lamb and chicken, served with celeriac and carrot salad.

Clean and chop carrots, grate the celeriac and mix together. Sprinkle with lemon juice. Toss in dressing.

Patricia McCowen's house appears to be always full. It has a lovely cosy atmosphere, a big open kitchen with a large wooden table in the centre, a bright red Aga and a vast fridge (she has no deep freeze). Everything is beautifully clean and tidy and her meals seem to appear as if by magic. She is never disturbed when extra people turn up for a meal without warning, and there is always a minimum of seven to feed.

'I find planning the menus the worst thing, but I like cooking. I use fresh vegetables and prefer plain roast meat, preferably on the bone, which has all the flavour, and which I am lucky enough to get as I live on a farm. I use my Magimix a great deal and also a Kenwood, which is wonderful for making soups.

'I don't mind people being in the kitchen when I'm cooking, in fact as a rule I enjoy their company; but when there's lots to be done I prefer to be on my own. So on Saturday and Sunday mornings I encourage my guests to stay in bed and have a breakfast tray – much easier than having the kitchen cluttered up with children and cigarettes and I can get a move on. But I will always cook a breakfast for those who want it – on Saturday probably eggs, sausages and bacon. On Sunday there may be cold ham, poached or boiled eggs, croissants and black cherry jam. And always lots of coffee.

'I am a fairly quick worker and prefer doing things at the last minute. I don't plan a weekend days in advance – I think about it on Thursday, unless I particularly want to test something, in which case I will try it out mid-week – but I do try to prepare as much as possible in advance.

The white wines that Patricia uses are: 1976 Gewürztraminer, Blanc de Blancs, Laurent Persier and Chianti Ruffino. Her red wines might be Fleurie, 1978 Louis La tour or Domaine de l'Eglise. After dinner there may be Calvados, (Au père ma gloire – age inconnu).

OCTOBER

*Armsworth Hill farmhouse was derelict*
*when the McCowens bought it nine years ago, and*
*they have entirely rebuilt it to their own*
*design. All of the rooms lead off an almost*
*circular galleried hall which has a marble floor*
*and a huge old church chandelier. The house*
*is rendered and painted white, and faces*
*on to a courtyard which used to be full of cattle.*
*Most of the yard is now occupied by a billiard*
*room, granny flat and garages; and in the*
*centre is a large round flower bed. The house*
*stands on top of a hill, which makes it very*
*light and sunny, and there are extensive*
*views over farmland to the south and west – the*
*best view of all being from the kitchen.*

# OCTOBER

---<>---

# Patricia McCowen

## Friday

**SUPPER**

Chicken Livers in Cream and Tomato Sauce

Stuffed Trout
Normandy Potatoes
Salad

Pears in Wine

## Saturday

**LUNCH**

Country Pâté and Hot French Bread
Mushroom, Walnut and Watercress Salad

Cheese
Fresh Fruit

**DINNER**

Fish Soup with Grapes

Roast Partridge
Sauté Potatoes cooked in Rosemary
Brussels Sprouts
Purée of Cauliflower

Chocolate Nut Cake

## Sunday

**LUNCH**

Roast Beef and Yorkshire Pudding
Roast Potatoes
Mashed Carrots and Swedes
Cabbage

French Apple Tart

**SUPPER**

Potted Shrimps

Cold Roast Beef or Omelettes

Cheese

# Friday Supper

(for 6 people)

## CHICKEN LIVERS IN CREAM WITH TOMATO SAUCE

275 ml *½ pint double cream*
275 g *10 oz chicken livers*
*3 eggs and 2 egg yolks*
*½ clove garlic*
*Salt and pepper*
*Pinch of grated nutmeg*

TOMATO SAUCE

*1 tablespoon butter*
*2 shallots, chopped*
*Clove of garlic, crushed*
1 kg *2 lb tomatoes*

Thoroughly butter 6 ramekins. Line a roasting tin with a tea towel. Half-fill with water.

Bring cream to the boil. Purée the chicken livers in blender with the eggs and egg yolks. Pour mixture into a bowl and add cream, slowly whisking all the time. Add garlic, season to taste and add the nutmeg. Spoon into the ramekins, filling not more than three-quarters full.*

Set the ramekins in the water bath and bring almost to simmering point on top of the stove. Transfer to oven and bake at 350°F 180°C gas 4, for 30–40 minutes or until a skewer inserted in the centre comes out clean. Remove from oven, keeping ramekins in water bath.

To make the tomato sauce, melt the butter, add the shallots and cook until soft but not coloured. Add the rest of the ingredients, season and simmer uncovered for 30–40 minutes until the tomatoes are soft. Purée the sauce and strain it; return to rinsed-out pan to reheat and reduce to a light coating consistency. Season to taste: it needs a lot of salt.*

To finish: turn out each ramekin and coat with sauce. Keep in warmer until required. Sprinkle with a little chopped basil to serve.

*Can be prepared in advance.

PREPARATION TIME 15 minutes.

## STUFFED TROUT

*6 trout*
*Seasoned flour*
175 g *6 oz butter*
*Juice of 1 lemon and 1 orange*
*1 tablespoon chopped parsley*

STUFFING

*4 shallots*
150 g *5 oz mushrooms, chopped*
*3 large handfuls fresh spinach, blanched*
*or*
500 g *1 lb packet frozen*
*1 tablespoon mixed herbs*
*Salt and pepper*

Bone the trout: first snip off the fins and vandyke the tail. Cut off the head and with a sharp knife slit down the back, keeping the knife on top of the back bone. Open up the fish until it lies flat and slip the knife under the bone at the head end and cut down to just about the tail. Lift out the bone.

To prepare stuffing: finely chop the shallots, soften them in 1–1½ oz (25–35 g) butter; add the mushrooms, spinach and herbs. Season, cover pan and simmer for 5–6 minutes. Leave to cool, then put into the trout. Reshape fish and roll carefully in seasoned flour.*

Fry the trout in butter until brown on both sides, turning once. Season with salt and ground pepper, dish up and keep warm.

# Friday Supper

## continued

GARNISH

*1 large orange*
*1 dessertspoon castor sugar*
*Few sprigs of watercress*
*Juice of 1 lemon*

Wipe out the pan, slice the orange and fry quickly in $\frac{1}{2}$ oz (12 g) butter, dusting with a little castor sugar to brown slightly; take out orange and keep warm. Wipe out pan and add 2 oz (50 g) butter. Cook until it is nut brown, then quickly add the lemon and orange juices and chopped parsley. Pour at once over the trout and surround with orange slices and watercress.

PREPARATION TIME 20 minutes to prepare fish; 30 minutes to finish.

*You can prepare the trout a day in advance. Cover with cling film and leave in fridge.

NORMANDY POTATOES

750 g   *1½ lb potatoes*
25 g   *1 oz butter*
275 ml   *½ pint milk*
*Seasoning*

Cut the potatoes into thin slices and arrange overlapping in a well buttered fireproof dish. Season between layers with salt and freshly ground black pepper. Pour over milk and cover with the remaining butter cut into small pieces. Bake in hot oven, 400°F 200°C gas 6, for about 50–60 minutes.

The potatoes may be peeled a few hours before and left in cold water.

## PEARS IN WINE

*6 small ripe dessert pears*
150 ml   *¼ pint water*
150 ml   *¼ pint claret or Burgundy*
150 g   *5 oz loaf sugar*
*Strip of lemon rind*
*Small piece of cinnamon stick*
*1 level teaspoon arrowroot*
25 g   *1 oz shredded almonds, toasted*

Shake the sugar in a pan with the wine, water and flavouring and dissolve slowly. Increase the heat and boil for 1 minute. Meanwhile peel the pears, leaving the stalks on but removing the eye from the bottoms, and place in the prepared syrup. The pears should sit upright in the syrup, so to hold them in position cut a disc of greaseproof paper the size of the stewpan and make a small hole for each stalk.

Cover the pan with a lid and poach the pears in a moderate oven until tender, but allow at least 20–30 minutes even if the pears are ripe, or they discolour around the core on standing.

Remove the pears from the pan, strain the syrup, check the quantity and reduce if necessary to $\frac{1}{2}$ pint (275 ml). Mix the arrowroot with a little water, add to the syrup, stir until boiling and cook until clear.

Arrange the pears in a serving dish, spoon over the wine sauce and scatter with toasted almonds. Serve cold with a bowl of whipped cream.

# Saturday Lunch

## (for 6 people)

### COUNTRY PATE (Serves 12)

450 g    *1 lb minced pork*
450 g    *1 lb minced veal*
225 g    *8 oz minced ham or bacon*
175 g    *6 oz pig's liver*
         *2 cloves garlic*
         *Salt and pepper*
         *Allspice*
         *1 glass brandy*
         *Slices of fat, unsmoked bacon*
         *1 bayleaf*
         *Unsalted butter*

Combine the minced meats and fat; remove all skin and ducts from the liver, pass through a mincer or blender and add to the mixture. Season with freshly ground black pepper and allspice, crush the garlic with salt and add with the brandy.

Line a terrine with bacon fat, press in the mixture, place a bay leaf on the top and then the lid. Seal down with a flour and water paste and cook in a *bain marie* for about 1½ hours in a moderate oven, 350°F 180°C gas 4. Press lightly until cold and pour over a little unsalted butter.

PREPARATION TIME 10–15 minutes if the meats are already minced.

This can be made several days in advance, and can be frozen.

Serve with hot French bread and mushroom, walnut and watercress salad.

### MUSHROOM, WALNUT AND WATERCRESS SALAD

         *1 bunch watercress*
         *1 head lettuce*
         *8–12 walnuts*
175 g    *4–6 oz mushrooms*
         *2 tablespoons chopped parsley*
         *2 tablespoons chopped chives*
         *Vinaigrette*

Wash and trim watercress; wash lettuce leaves and dry. Shell and halve walnuts. Wipe mushrooms, trim stem ends and slice thinly. Line a salad bowl with lettuce, arrange watercress in the centre. Scatter nuts and mushrooms over them, together with vinaigrette and herbs. Toss salad just before serving.

Follow with cheese and fruit.

# Saturday Dinner

## (for 8 people)

---

### FISH SOUP WITH GRAPES

675 g   *1½ lb filleted fresh haddock*
*2 medium onions, chopped*
*3 tomatoes, skinned*
150 g   *5 oz butter*
50 g   *2 oz flour*
225 g   *8 oz prawns or shrimps, peeled*
225 g   *8 oz grapes, peeled and stoned*
275 ml   *½ pint cream*
*Bouquet garni*

Skin the fish and simmer it in 2½ pints (1½ litres) water with the skin (for flavour), a bouquet garni and seasoning for 6–10 minutes only. Remove fish and flake. Sauté the chopped onions in butter, add chopped tomatoes and flour, then add all the stock, fish and shrimps.*

Simmer a little longer; add grapes and cream just before serving and reheat but do not boil. Sprinkle with chopped basil or parsley.

PREPARATION TIME Approximately 25 minutes.

*May be made a day in advance.

### ROAST PARTRIDGE

*1 partridge per person*

Cover breast of partridge with butter and a rasher of fat bacon, place in roasting tin with a little red wine. Roast for approximately 20 minutes at 425°F 220°C gas 7. Take up and make clear gravy. Garnish with watercress.

FRIED BREADCRUMBS Make 8 tablespoons of fresh breadcrumbs and fry in 2 oz (50 g) butter for about 4 minutes until golden. Drain excess butter and keep warm.

SAUTÉ POTATOES Chop up cooked potatoes and sauté in butter with a little rosemary.

BRUSSELS SPROUTS Prepare sprouts and put in saucepan, add boiling water and salt. Bring back to the boil and boil for a few more minutes, drain, add butter and dish up. (I hate over-cooked sprouts!)

PUREE OF CAULIFLOWER

*1 medium cauliflower*
*Salt and pepper*
25 g   *1 oz butter*
*Grated nutmeg*
*1–2 tablespoons cream*

Divide the cauliflower into florets. Cook them in boiling salted water for 10 minutes or until just tender. Drain very thoroughly and purée in a blender. Melt the butter, add the purée with the nutmeg, salt and pepper and cook, stirring until very hot. Stir in the cream and dish up.

I cook all this on Saturday evening, having prepared the vegetables and put them in plastic bags in the fridge on Friday.

---

### CHOCOLATE NUT CAKE

This should be made a day in advance.

Grease and flour 2 9-inch (22-cm) tins and line with Bakewell paper; set oven at 350°F 180°C gas 4.

Whip the egg whites with a pinch of salt to a really firm snow, then gradually add the castor sugar, continuing to whisk until it stands in peaks. Brown the hazelnuts by baking for 5–6 minutes in a hot oven, rub them briskly in a rough cloth to remove the skins, then grind the kernels in a Magimix or liquidizer. Fold the nuts into the whites with the vinegar and vanilla, turn into prepared tins. Bake in the pre-heated oven for 35 minutes. Remove and leave in tins for a few minutes before turning out.

Break up or grate the chocolate, put it in a pan with the water and stir over a gentle heat until the chocolate has dissolved. Add the sugar and boil gently with the pan uncovered for about 15 minutes. Pour off the chocolate into a bowl, dust with castor sugar, cover with dampened greaseproof paper to prevent skin forming and leave to get cold.

Lightly whip the cream and fold in 2–3 tablespoons of chocolate sauce to flavour it well. Spread this on one half of the cake, place the other half on top and press together lightly. Leave the cake overnight in the refrigerator or chill for several hours, then dust the top with icing sugar and decorate with extra whipped cream. Serve with the rest of the chocolate sauce.

PREPARATION TIME 40 minutes.

6 egg whites
Pinch of salt
375 g  13 oz castor sugar
300 g  7 oz hazelnuts
1½ teaspoons vinegar
2–3 drops vanilla essence

FILLING

275 ml  ½ pint double cream

CHOCOLATE SAUCE

225 g  8 oz plain chocolate
350 ml  12 fl oz water
150 g  5 oz granulated sugar

DECORATION

Icing sugar
Whipped cream

# Sunday Lunch

## (for 6–8 people)

### ROAST BEEF AND YORKSHIRE PUDDING

| | |
|---|---|
| 4 kg | *3 ribs of beef on the bone, approximately 9 lb* |

This will be sufficient beef for up to 8 people, and you will have some left over for Sunday supper. Roast it at 400°F 200°C gas 6 for 15 minutes to the pound (450 g) if you like it rare; longer if you prefer it well done.

HORSE-RADISH SAUCE

*3 roots of horse-radish
or
1¼–2 tablespoons of fresh grated horse-radish
1 teaspoon powdered English mustard
1 dessertspoon malt vinegar
Sugar to taste
Salt and pepper*
275 ml *½ pint cream*

You can buy fresh grated horse-radish, if you haven't any in your garden.

Peel and roughly chop horse-radish. Chop finely in grinder attachment of blender. Put into basin, add vinegar, mustard, sugar, salt and pepper. Pour on the cream and stir gently to mix. With hand beater whip very gently until slightly thick. Cover and leave in fridge until needed.

Can be made a day in advance.

YORKSHIRE PUDDING

175 g *6 oz plain flour*
*2 eggs*
275 ml *½ pint milk and water mixed*
*A little salt*

Put flour, salt, eggs and little liquid in Magimix or liquidizer and blend. Add rest of liquid and blend once again. Leave to rest until needed. Put a little dripping into individual cake tins and melt. Pour in mixture and cook in hot oven, 425°F 220°C gas 7, for about 35 minutes.

ROAST POTATOES Cover with cold water and bring to the boil; after a few minutes drain, when cool scrape with a fork and leave on kitchen paper until needed. (Do not leave for too long otherwise they discolour.) Heat fat in tin and roast at the bottom of a hot oven, 425°F 220°C gas 7, for 50–60 minutes.

MASHED CARROTS AND SWEDES Peel swedes and cut into smallish pieces. Peel carrots, cut up and add to swedes. Cover with cold water and bring to the boil. Cook for approximately 20 minutes or until soft. Drain and mash. Add salt, black pepper, butter and dish up.

CABBAGE Put shredded cabbage into a saucepan with some salt. Pour on boiling water, bring back to the boil, boil for a few seconds and drain. Place on serving dish, dot with butter and black pepper.

I cover vegetables with either wet greaseproof paper or foil or both and place in warmer until needed.

### FRENCH APPLE TART

**PATE SUCRE**

125 g    *4 oz plain flour*
50 g    *2 oz butter*
50 g    *2 oz castor sugar*
        *2 egg yolks*
        *2 drops vanilla essence*

**FILLING**

450 g    *1 lb apples*
        *3 heaped tablespoons*
          *apricot jam*
        *Squeeze of lemon*

Sift flour with a pinch of salt on to a pastry board, make a well in the centre and in this place the other ingredients. Using finger tips of one hand work only the butter, sugar and yolks together, then quickly draw in the flour and knead lightly until smooth. Wrap in foil and chill for at least 1 hour before using.*

Line a 7-inch (18-cm) flan ring with the pastry and prick bottom lightly. Peel and quarter the apples, remove the core and slice thinly. Arrange the slices overlapping in circles to fill the flan. Dust the top layer only with a little sugar and bake in a moderate oven, 350°F 180°C gas 4, for 20–30 minutes.

Meanwhile heat the jam with the lemon until runny, then strain. When the flan is cooked, remove ring and brush the top and sides with the glaze.

*I make the pâte sucré the day before.

# Sunday Supper

(for 2 people)

Potted shrimps, cold roast beef or omelettes and cheese

# Toby Eady

---

|          | |
|----------|---|
| *Friday* | **SUPPER** |
|          | Spaghetti Putari |
|          | Endive Salad |
|          | Fresh Cheddar with Bath Oliver Biscuits |

|            | |
|------------|---|
| *Saturday* | **LUNCH** |
|            | Baked Fillets of Plaice |
|            | Green Cabbage |
|            | Cheddar |

**DINNER**

Leeks in Vinaigrette

Venison and Oxtail Stew
Mashed Potatoes
Winter Salad

Mushroom Savoury

|          | |
|----------|---|
| *Sunday* | **LUNCH** |
|          | Chinese Goose with a Salad Stuffing |
|          | Roast Turnips |
|          | Brie and Biscuits |

**SUPPER**

Lentil Stew

# Friday Supper

## (for 6 people)

### SPAGHETTI PUTARI

| | |
|---|---|
| 50 g | *1 tin anchovies, chopped finely* |
| | *20 black olives, split* |
| 400 g | *14 oz tin tomatoes* |
| | *8 cloves of garlic* |
| | *Cayenne pepper* |
| 100 g | *4 oz capers* |
| | *Olive oil* |
| 750 g | *1½ lb spaghetti, fresh if possible* |

This is a Neapolitan dish which was served to pimps by their whores to keep them warm while they were working.

Cook the anchovies with the olives in olive oil until they are nearly a paste, then add the tin of tomatoes without juice, the capers and chopped garlic and sprinkle on a little cayenne. Let it fry and bubble for a few minutes.

Cook the spaghetti *al dente* in boiling salted water with a spoonful of olive oil for approximately 12 minutes (if it is fresh it will take only half as long). Then tip the spaghetti into the sauce, toss and serve in a large warmed bowl.

### ENDIVE SALAD

*4 endives*
*4 tablespoons olive oil*
*1 tablespoon tarragon*
  *vinegar*
*1 bay leaf, crushed*
*Salt and pepper*
*1 teaspoon mustard*
*Pinch of sugar*

Chop the endive and mix with the vinaigrette.

Fresh Cheddar cheese, preferably a local one, with Bath Oliver biscuits.

# Saturday Lunch

## (for 6 people)

### BAKED FILLETS OF PLAICE

*6 fillets of plaice*
*Butter*
*2 lemons*

Rub the plaice with butter, put in an ovenproof dish already rubbed with butter, and place in a hot oven, 450°F 230°C gas 8, for about 12 minutes. Serve with wedges of lemons.

GREEN CABBAGE Chop the cabbage and put in a pan with ½ inch (1 cm) of boiling water. Cook for 30 minutes. Sprinkle with a little crushed red pepper.

Follow by Cheddar cheese.

# Saturday Dinner

## (for 8 people)

### LEEKS VINAIGRETTE

*3 small leeks per person*
*Vinaigrette (see page 38)*

Boil leeks till just done, about 12 minutes, then let cool and serve with a vinaigrette with a bay leaf crushed into it.

### VENISON AND OXTAIL STEW

*1 large oxtail*
500 g *1 lb diced venison*
*2 stalks of celery*
*4 carrots*
*2 small onions*
*2 leeks*
*1 small turnip or parsnip*
*A small handful of juniper*
  *berries*
*4 black peppercorns*
*2 bay leaves*
*Coriander seeds*
*Salt*
75 ml *½ bottle coarse red wine*
*½ tumbler Calvados/Armagnac*
275 ml *1 can game soup or bouillon*

This is a particularly good way to cook venison because it soaks up the juices and flavour from the oxtail. This dish can never be overcooked as long as there is plenty of liquid.

Take a large casserole and place the oxtail with the chopped vegetables in the bottom. Add the bay leaves, juniper berries, coriander seeds and peppercorns and cover with the soup. Add the venison, salt and wine and place in a low oven, 200°F 100°C gas ¼, for 3 hours. Add the Calvados and return to oven for a further hour. Remove from the oven, skim off the fat and put back in a hot oven for 10–15 minutes. Serve.

Serve with mashed potatoes.

WINTER SALAD Chopped celery, apples, walnuts and watercress mixed in a vinaigrette made with oil, lemon and salt.

### MUSHROOM SAVOURY

500 g *1 lb button mushrooms*
*8 slices of bread*
*Butter*

Wash the mushrooms, cook in butter for a few minutes and pile them on to hot toast.

# Sunday Lunch

(for 6 people)

### CHINESE GOOSE WITH A SALAD STUFFING

$3\frac{3}{4}$ kg *8 lb dressed goose*
*1 red cabbage, chopped*
*2 nuts stem ginger, chopped*
*4 sticks celery, chopped*
*3 eating apples, cored and*
  *chopped*
*Pine kernels*
*1 orange rind cut in*
  *julienne strips*
*Coriander seeds*
*1 clove of garlic, crushed*
*Ground nutmeg*

Parboil the goose for 10 minutes, holding it by the legs. If you do this you will not need to drain the bird repeatedly while roasting. Combine all the other ingredients and stuff the goose. Roast it with no fat for $1\frac{1}{2}$ hours in a hot oven, 450°F 230°C gas 8. Drain it once during the cooking time and baste it once to get the skin crisp.

Serve with roasted white turnips cooked with caraway seeds and mustard oil in a hot oven for about 40 minutes.

# Sunday Supper

(for 2 people)

### LENTIL STEW

*2 handfuls of lentils*
*3 turnips*
*1 stick of celery*
*1 chicken stock cube*
*1 leek*

This is a very good way of using up left overs when you have to go back to London on Sunday night.

Soak lentils overnight with salt. Drain, then cook in a large saucepan with any left overs from the oxtail stew and goose and celery stuffing. Chop the turnips, celery and leeks, add a chicken stock cube and enough water to cover. Let it cook slowly, drying up. Serve moist.

# NOVEMBER

## Margaret Read

Queen Manor was originally built as a pair of cottages or a small farmhouse in the early eighteenth century, and enlarged circa 1820. The north range, seen through the gateway, is of red brick in Flemish bond with a plinth and platband, now painted. Early in the nineteenth century the front of the house was rebuilt in local white brick; and probably at the same time the part not shown in the picture was rebuilt in the bonded red brick and flint characteristic of Wiltshire. In the garden is an icehouse, probably built in the late eighteenth century.

# SHOOTING WEEKEND

### Friday

**SUPPER**

Fish Mousse

Hot Tongue with Pickled Walnut Sauce
Roast Potatoes
Sea Kale

Cheese and Biscuits
Smoked Oyster Savoury

### Saturday

**LUNCH**

Leek Soup

Steak and Kidney Casserole
Potatoes in Jackets
Green Salad

English Cheese
Apples

**DINNER**

Mushroom and Prawn Salad

Wild Duck and Green Olive Sauce
Roast Potatoes
Petit Pois

Orange and Grape Compôte

### Sunday

**LUNCH**

Boiled Beef and Dumplings
Potatoes Lyonnaise
Sprouting Broccoli

Apple Compôte
Cheese and Celery

# Friday Supper
## (for 6 people)

### FISH MOUSSE

| | |
|---|---|
| 225 g | *8 oz Finnan haddock* |
| 275 ml | *½ pint milk* |
| | *2 tablespoons smoked salmon trimmings cut into strips* |
| 175 g | *6 oz peeled prawns* |
| | *3 hard-boiled eggs, chopped* |
| 275 ml | *½ pint aspic (see instructions on packet)* |
| | *1 tablespoon chopped parsley* |
| 150 ml | *¼ pint double cream* |
| | *1 tablespoon flour* |
| | *Salt and pepper* |
| | *1 tablespoon butter* |
| | *Freshly grated nutmeg* |
| | *Juice of 1 small lemon* |

Cook the haddock in milk with an onion, bay leaf, peppercorns etc. for approximately 10 minutes. Keep milk.

Melt the butter in a saucepan and stir in the flour off the heat. Add the fish milk, pepper and nutmeg (check to see if it needs salt). Beat the cream and add to the sauce when it has cooled. Add the aspic, saving a little, and the lemon juice. Finally, add the flaked fish, smoked salmon, prawns, eggs and parsley and turn into a soufflé dish. When cold decorate with the rest of the aspic.

This can be made a day in advance.

PREPARATION TIME 30 minutes.

### HOT TONGUE WITH PICKLED WALNUT SAUCE

| | |
|---|---|
| 1¼ kg | *2¼–2½ lb ox tongue (fresh or pickled)* |
| | *1 carrot, sliced* |
| | *1 onion, sliced* |
| | *1 stalk of celery, chopped* |
| | *12 peppercorns* |
| | *2 cloves* |
| | *Herbs: thyme, parsley etc.* |
| | **SAUCE** |
| | *1 tablespoon butter* |
| | *1 dessertspoon flour* |
| 275 ml | *½ pint chicken stock* |
| | *1 teaspoon English mustard* |
| | *1 tablespoon white wine vinegar* |
| | *2 tablespoons red wine* |
| | *4 pickled walnuts, chopped* |
| | *2 tablespoons chopped parsley* |
| | **SEA KALE** |
| 750 g | *about 1½ lb* |

Fill a large pan with cold water and all the ingredients. Cover and simmer for about 3 hours. Remove the tongues, peel, slice and arrange on a serving dish. Keep warm.

Melt the butter in a saucepan and stir in the flour off the heat. Return to heat and let it brown a little, stir in the stock, mustard, vinegar to taste and the wine.

Stir the sauce until it is smooth and thick, then add the parsley and chopped walnuts. Cover with greaseproof paper and keep warm if not eating immediately.

Serve with roast potatoes (see page 31).

Remove tops and cook like spinach. Wash and trim the stalks then blanch in boiling salted water to which a little lemon juice has been added for 20–30 minutes, according to age and size. Drain, put on a serving dish and pour over a little melted butter. Keep warm.

Follow by cheese and biscuits.

### SMOKED OYSTER SAVOURY

*6 slices thin white bread*
*    with crusts removed*
*6 rashers streaky bacon*
*12 smoked oysters*
*Oil*

Cut the bread into 12 1½-inch (4-cm) squares. Fry in oil and when golden remove and drain on kitchen paper. Cut the rinds off the bacon and halve. Wrap up each oyster in a piece of bacon. Fry quickly and dry.

These can be prepared before dinner and warmed up during the main course.

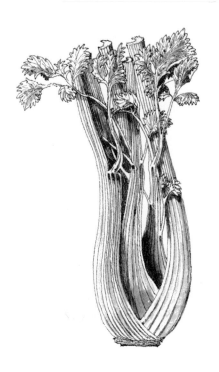

# Saturday Lunch

## (for 6 people)

### LEEK SOUP

| | |
|---|---|
| 1 kg | *2 lb leeks* |
| | *2 medium onions* |
| 75 g | *3 oz butter* |
| | *3 medium potatoes* |
| 1150 ml | *2 pints chicken stock* |
| | *1 level teaspoon salt* |
| | *Pepper* |
| 150 ml | *¼ pint single cream* |
| | *2 tablespoons chopped parsley* |

Roughly chop the vegetables. Melt the butter in a saucepan and add the vegetables. Stir gently for 10 minutes until soft but not brown. Add the stock, bring to the boil and simmer for 30 minutes. Cool and liquidize. Check seasoning.* Reheat and add the cream and parsley for decoration.

*This can be made a day in advance.

PREPARATION AND COOKING TIME 50 minutes.

### STEAK AND KIDNEY CASSEROLE

| | |
|---|---|
| 1 kg | *2 lb skirt of beef* |
| 500 g | *1 lb ox kidney, chopped* |
| | *A little plain flour* |
| | *2 shallots, finely chopped* |
| | *1 dessertspoon chopped* |
| | *parsley* |
| 425 ml | *¾ pint beef stock* |
| | *Salt and pepper* |

This is greatly improved if made a day in advance and reheated.

Cut steak into 1½-inch (4-cm) squares. Season the flour and roll the steak and kidney in it. Put in a casserole. Sprinkle with shallots and parsley. Pour over the stock and cook in a hot oven, 450°F 230°C gas 8, for ½ hour, then turn down the heat to 350°F 180°C gas 4, for 1½ hours.

Serve with potatoes in jackets, baked in hot oven for 1 hour, and a green salad, made with anything available in the garden.

Follow by English cheese and apples.

# Saturday Dinner

## (for 8 people)

### MUSHROOM AND PRAWN SALAD

450 g   *1 lb button mushrooms,*
     *thinly sliced*
     *10 tablespoons olive oil*
     *2 tablespoons white wine*
     *vinegar*
     *3 tablespoons lemon juice*
     *2 cloves garlic, crushed*
225 g   *8 oz shelled prawns*
     *3 tablespoons chopped parsley*
     *Pepper*
     *Sea salt*

Put the mushrooms into a shallow serving dish. Blend the olive oil, vinegar, lemon juice, garlic, pepper and salt. Pour over the mushrooms and chill.\* Just before serving, add the prawns, sprinkle with a little sea salt and chopped parsley, adding a little more oil if too dry.

\*Can be prepared in advance.

PREPARATION TIME 10 minutes.

### WILD DUCK AND GREEN OLIVE SAUCE

     *4 mallard*
     *3 tablespoons white*
     *breadcrumbs*
     *18 black olives, stoned*
     *24 green olives, stoned*
     *and halved*
     *Parsley*
     *2 medium onions*
125 g   *4 oz mushrooms*
     *6 rashers streaky bacon,*
     *rinded*
225 g   *8 oz butter*
     *1 rounded tablespoon flour*
     *Salt and pepper*
425 ml   *¾ pint duck or chicken stock*
     *3 tablespoons dry white wine*

Fry the onions in 3 oz (75 g) of the butter until soft. Add the bacon, also fry until soft. Add the mushrooms, black olives, parsley and breadcrumbs. Season with pepper only and stuff the ducks.

Cover the ducks with foil and cook them in a hot oven, 400°F 200°C gas 6, for 45 minutes with a little oil and butter. Remove foil for the last 10 minutes to let the birds brown. Put the birds on a serving dish, pour off the fat from the pan and add the juices to the sauce.

Make a brown roux with the remaining butter and the flour. Stir in the stock. Add the wine and stir until the sauce is smooth and fairly thick. Add the green olives. Cover with greaseproof paper and keep in warmer, or double boiler.

Serve with roast potatoes (see page 31), and petit pois from the deep freeze.

### ORANGE AND GRAPE COMPOTE

     *8 juicy oranges*
350 g   *12 oz green grapes*
350 g   *12 oz black grapes*
225 g   *8 oz castor sugar*
150 ml   *¼ pint water*
     *Juice of 1 lemon*
     *1 tablespoon Cointreau*

Cover the oranges with boiling water and allow to stand for 5 minutes. Drain and skin, removing all the pith. Slice thinly. Place on a serving dish. Halve and de-pip the grapes and arrange attractively on the oranges. Heat the sugar and water in a saucepan. Simmer for 1 minute and add the lemon juice. Allow to cool, add the Cointreau. Pour over the fruit and chill. (You may not need all of the syrup.)

This can be prepared a day in advance.

PREPARATION TIME 25 minutes.

# Sunday Lunch

## (for 6 people)

### BOILED BEEF AND DUMPLINGS

3 kg *6 lb salted silverside*
*2 large carrots*
*2 leeks*
*1 bay leaf*
*10 black peppercorns*
*3 cloves*
*Parsley*
450 g *1 lb shallots*
450 g *1 lb baby carrots*

Bring a large pan of water to the boil. Put in the meat, return to the boil and skim. Add the 2 large carrots, leeks, bay leaf, peppercorns, cloves and parsley and simmer gently for 30 minutes to lb (450 g).

Half an hour before serving add the baby carrots and skinned shallots. When cooked remove the meat on to a serving dish and surround with the baby carrots and shallots. Keep warm. Keep the water to cook the dumplings in.

#### DUMPLINGS

125 g *4 oz chopped suet*
225 g *8 oz self-raising flour*
*Pinch of salt*
150 ml *Teacup of cold water*

Prepare the dumpling mixture while the meat is boiling.

Sift the flour with the salt. Add the suet and mix well. Moisten with the water to make a light dough. Divide into small pieces, roll up and drop them into the boiling water the meat was cooked in. Cover and simmer for 15 minutes.

#### POTATOES LYONNAISE

*1 medium potato per person*
*1 clove garlic*
425 ml *¾ pint cream*
*Salt and pepper*

Grease a flat earthenware dish with butter and rub a clove of garlic round the edge. Peel and thinly slice the potatoes. Put one layer in the dish, season, then more potatoes, etc. Pour in the cream and bake in a medium oven, 350°F 180°C gas 4, for 2–2¼ hours.

Serve with sprouting broccoli.

### APPLE COMPOTE

1 kg *2 lb Bramley apples*
50 g *2 oz butter*
*Freshly grated rind and juice of 1 lemon*
175 g *6 oz demarara sugar*

Peel and thinly slice the apples. Grease a large shallow baking dish with butter. Arrange the apples over the base of the dish and sprinkle with lemon rind and sugar. Pour over the lemon juice. Add the remaining butter cut into pieces. Cook, uncovered, in the centre of a medium oven, 350°F 180°C gas 4, while eating the main course.

Serve with a large jug of fresh cream.

# Sunday Supper

Baked Eggs (see page 123)

# Georgia Langton

## Friday

SUPPER

Baked Mushrooms with Garlic and Parsley Butter
Granary Bread

Pork Chops flavoured with Juniper Berries
Lentils with Diced Carrots

## Saturday

LUNCH

Beef Stew with Black Olives
Boiled Potatoes

Winter Fruit Salad with Red Wine and Honey Sauce

DINNER

Home Made Potted Shrimps

Guinea Fowl, Chicken or Pheasant with Cèpe Mushroom Sauce
Julienne of Carrots, Onion and Celery

Stilton, Pear, Watercress and Walnut Salad

## Sunday

LUNCH

Lamb flavoured with Coriander Seeds
Stirred Spinach
Potatoes and Onions

Strong Cheddar
Blue Cheshire
Home-Made Pickled Blackberries

SUPPER

Leek and Potato Soup
Pheasant Legs or Sausages
Sweet and Sour Red Cabbage
Baked Potatoes

# Friday Supper

## (for 6 people)

---

### BAKED MUSHROOMS WITH GARLIC AND PARSLEY BUTTER

|         |                                  |
|---------|----------------------------------|
|         | *4 or 5 large white mushrooms per person* |
| 500 g   | *1 lb unsalted butter*           |
|         | *2 cloves garlic*                |
|         | *4 tablespoons chopped parsley*  |
|         | *Black pepper and salt*          |
|         | *Lemon*                          |

Having softened the butter, add crushed garlic, parsley, large amount of black pepper and mix well. Take stalks out of mushrooms, sprinkle with few drops of lemon juice and fill each centre with the 'snail butter'. Leave till ready to cook.*

Put mushrooms on to baking dish or snail plates if you have them. Bake in a very hot oven, 450°F 230°C gas 8, for about 8 minutes or until butter has melted and mushrooms are cooked. The mushrooms are much better slightly underdone than flabby. Sprinkle with salt and serve immediately with large chunks of granary bread to soak up the buttery juice. (Do not salt the mushrooms *before* cooking as it makes all the juice come out.)

*Can be done in the morning or day before.

### PORK CHOPS FLAVOURED WITH JUNIPER BERRIES

|         |                                  |
|---------|----------------------------------|
|         | *6 large pork chops, not too thick* |
|         | *1½ tablespoons juniper berries* |
|         | *Garlic*                         |
| 75 ml   | *Olive oil (about coffee cupful)* |
|         | *Black pepper and salt*          |

Crush the juniper berries and slice the garlic into slivers. Score each chop lightly and insert sliver of garlic into each chop near the bone and press in the crushed berries. Add a good deal of roughly ground black pepper and pour over a film of good olive oil. Leave to marinade in ovenproof dish they are to be cooked and served in.* Heat grill till very hot and cook chops till done. Sprinkle well with salt and serve.

*Prepare in morning.

|         | **LENTILS**                      |
|---------|----------------------------------|
| 275 g   | *10 oz green lentils*            |
| 130 g   | *5 oz carrots, diced*           |
| 130 g   | *5 oz onion, diced*             |
|         | *Salt and pepper*               |
|         | *Bouquet garni (must include bay leaf)* |
|         | *Parsley*                        |
|         | *Olive oil*                      |

Rinse the lentils – they will not need soaking – and cover with cold water. Bring to the boil and add the diced carrots and onions, the bouquet garni and salt. Cook covered fairly gently for about ½ hour or until they are tender. Drain. Pour on some olive oil as if for a salad and sprinkle with parsley. Serve on very hot plates with juice from the pork chops poured over the top of the lentils.

These lentils are also delicious cold, eaten as a salad with a nice strong vinaigrette.

---

# *Saturday Lunch*

## (for 6 people)

### BEEF STEW WITH BLACK OLIVES

2 kg  *4 lb topside beef*
*8 tablespoons brandy*
*½ bottle red wine*
*2 cloves garlic, crushed*
*Thyme, bay leaf and parsley*
*Small strip of orange peel*
275 g  *10 oz black olives, stoned*

These quantities are enough for at least 8 people but the stew when cooked can be kept frozen.

Cut meat into cubes about 1 in (2 cm) square and brown in olive oil and butter. Warm brandy, pour over meat and flame it. Add red wine, orange rind and herbs, season with black pepper and not too much salt and cook covered in a slow oven, 250–300°F, 140–150°C gas 1–2, for 3 to 4 hours.* Just before serving add the black olives and adjust seasoning.

*Can be made in advance.

Serve with plain boiled potatoes cooked in their skins.

### WINTER FRUIT SALAD WITH RED WINE AND HONEY SAUCE

*1 melon*
*2 pears*
*2 apples*
225 g  *8 oz green grapes*
*2 bananas*
*1 grapefruit*
275 ml  *½ pint red Bordeaux*
150 ml  *¼ pint water*
*1 vanilla pod*
*4 tablespoons heather honey*
*or any other good honey*

This salad can of course be made at any time of the year with a selection of different fruits. This combination is very pretty because all the fruit is white.

Put wine into pan and reduce by fast boiling by half, then add the water, honey and split vanilla pod and bring back to the boil. Cool and chill in fridge.*
  I never peel the fruit but simply chop it up and chill an hour or so before the meal. Pour the sauce over just before serving.

*Can be made the day before.

# Saturday Dinner
## (for 8 people)

### HOME-MADE POTTED SHRIMPS

750 g   *1½ lb frozen prawns*
500 g   *1 lb unsalted butter*
          *Mixed spice*
          *Black pepper*
          *Cayenne pepper*
          *Salt*
          *Juice of 1½ lemons*
          *Lemon rind, thinly sliced*
             *and blanched*

This should be prepared the day before.

Unfreeze the prawns in a sieve – the watery juices are not wanted. When thawed squeeze the lemon juice over them. Melt half the butter very gently and add the prawns, mixed spice, black pepper and cayenne, salt and blanched lemon rinds. Heat prawns through – do not try to cook them. Put a spoonful at the bottom of eight individual ramekin dishes. Allow to cool and set slightly in the fridge. Then cover each dish with the remaining butter. Chill overnight.

TO SERVE do not turn out. Serve with a ramekin on each plate, plus some hot toast and extra lemon.

### GUINEA FOWL, CHICKEN OR PHEASANT WITH CEPE SAUCE

2 × 1½ kg   *2 × 3 lb guinea fowl,*
           *chicken or pheasant*
          *⅓ bottle good dry white*
           *wine*
150 ml   *¼ pint good chicken stock*
850 ml   *1½ pints double cream*
          *Salt and pepper*
          *2 egg yolks if necessary*
          *Unsalted butter*
20 gm   *¾ oz dried mushrooms*
           *(cèpes if possible)*

Soak the *cèpes* for ½ hour in warm water. In an ovenproof dish large enough to hold both birds, brown in butter gently, taking care not to burn the butter. Add the wine and stock and reduce the liquid by one third. Then finish off cooking the birds in the oven at 350°F 180°C gas 4, for about 20 minutes per lb (450 g). They will cook further in the sauce so it will not hurt if they are still slightly pink. Remove and carve and keep warm in serving dish.

    While birds are cooking, drain the *cèpes*, slice roughly and cook gently in butter. Keep warm.

TO MAKE SAUCE Reheat the liquid in which the birds were cooked. Add the double cream and the *cèpes* and reduce till thick enough to coat the back of a spoon. If you have no time to do this you can thicken the sauce by beating the egg yolks into it away from the heat. Test for seasoning. Pour sauce over chicken and keep warm.

JULIENNE OF CARROTS, ONIONS AND CELERY Good handful per person of a mixture of these three vegetables, washed, peeled and cut into julienne strips approximately $\frac{1}{8}$ inch (2 mm) wide by 2 inches (5 cm) long.

These can be prepared in the morning and kept in the fridge in a bowl with a damp drying up cloth over them.

Heat a very small amount of butter in a large sauté pan and add the vegetables. Season liberally with salt and pepper and cook very quickly over fairly high heat, turning the vegetables all the time. They should not take more than 5 or 6 minutes as it is very important to have them still slightly crunchy. Serve as quickly as possible.

## STILTON SERVED WITH PEAR, WATERCRESS AND WALNUT SALAD

**WALNUT SALAD**

*1 pear per person, peeled and sliced*
*1 slice of good Stilton per person*
*2 bunches of watercress*
*Handful of walnuts*

VINAIGRETTE SAUCE Put 1 dessertspoon good French mustard into bowl, season with salt and black pepper. Add 3 dessertspoons wine vinegar and stir well. Add good olive oil slowly as for a mayonnaise and finally flavour with 1 tablespoon walnut oil. The sauce should be thick just like a mayonnaise. Pour over the watercress at the last moment and toss well. (This sauce can be made in a Magimix or liquidizer.)

On each plate lay a slice of Stilton, a sliced pear and a small amount of watercress salad. Finally add a few whole walnuts. There should be no need for biscuits and butter but they can always be put on the table for guests to help themselves.

# Sunday Lunch

## (for 6 people)

### LAMB FLAVOURED WITH CORIANDER SEEDS

2–2½ kg · *4–5 lb shoulder of lamb on the bone*
*2 tablespoons crushed coriander seeds*
*Pepper and salt*
*Garlic cut into slivers*
*Unsalted butter*
150 ml · *Small cupful chicken stock*
150 ml · *¼ pint white wine*

Make 1-inch (2-cm) incisions into the meat, into which pop a small amount of the crushed coriander seeds and a sliver of garlic. Season liberally with salt and pepper and dot with butter. Lay in large baking tin.

VEGETABLES for each person: 2 potatoes and ½ onion, all peeled and cut into ¼-inch (5 mm) slices.

Surround the meat with the sliced vegetables, making sure to season the vegetables well. Cook in a hot oven, 400–450°F 220–230°C gas 7–8, for 20 minutes or until the top of the meat has taken colour. Remove from oven, pour over the wine and chicken stock. Finish cooking in a cooler oven, 300–350°F 170–180°C gas 3–4. This will take about 1 hour for a 4-lb leg, and an hour and 20 minutes for a 5-lb leg.

### STIRRED SPINACH

*2 large handfuls spinach or spinach beet per person*
125 g · *4 oz unsalted butter*

Wash the spinach. If using beet remove tough centre stalk. Put into large saucepan, sprinkle with salt and cover. Cook over moderate heat, without adding any water, till volume of spinach has reduced by half and all the water has come out of it. Drain and squeeze out any excess water by hand.*

Melt the unsalted butter in the pan and reheat the spinach very slowly, making sure it does not stick. Season with black pepper and serve.

*Can be done well in advance.

### PICKLED BLACKBERRIES

1½ kg · *3 lb freshly picked blackberries*
500 g · *1 lb sugar*
275 ml · *½ pint wine vinegar*
*½ teaspoon each cinnamon and ground cloves*

Simmer vinegar, sugar and spices together for 5 minutes. Add the blackberries and simmer for 10 minutes. Bottle and seal while hot. Delicious with cheese. Keeps very well.

Serve with strong Cheddar.

# Sunday Supper

(for 2 people)

### LEEK AND POTATO SOUP

*5 good-sized leeks, washed and roughly chopped*
*3 potatoes, peeled and roughly chopped*
75 g   *3 oz unsalted butter*
*Thyme*
*1 bay leaf*
*Black pepper and salt*
*Chicken stock (a cube will do)*
*Parsley, finely chopped*

This should *not* be a smooth dinner party soup: it is a rough 'country style' soup but is no less delicious for being unsophisticated.

Melt the butter and add the leeks. Cover the pan and sweat the leeks until soft (about 5 minutes). Add the potatoes, herbs and seasoning and just cover with chicken stock. Cook covered for approximately 15 minutes or until the potatoes are soft. Mash the soup with a potato masher in order to break up the cooked potatoes slightly. Finally sprinkle with parsley, add an extra knob or two of butter and serve.

### SWEET AND SOUR RED CABBAGE
(This serves 6 people)

*½ red cabbage, finely chopped*
*1 onion, roughly chopped*
*2 eating apples, peeled and chopped*
150 ml   *Cupful of wine vinegar*
*Mixed spice*
*Black pepper and salt*
*1 tablespoon sugar*

Put all the ingredients into a large ovenproof casserole. Heat on top till vinegar has boiled. Put on the lid and cook in moderate to slow oven, 250–300°F 140–150°C gas 1–3, for 1½–2 hours. This is even better when reheated.

Serve with either the pheasant legs left over from Saturday dinner or some good grilled pork sausages or a good boiling sausage. And baked potatoes, 1 per person, scrubbed, covered liberally with salt and cooked in hot oven for a good hour. We like our baked potatoes with very hard crunchy skins – hence the hot oven.

*The village of Colemore was mentioned in the Domesday Book in 1086. Colemore House, formerly the Rectory, dates from the early seventeenth century, with a major addition made at the end of the eighteenth century. It is built of whitened brick under a slate roof.*

# DECEMBER

## Noni de Zoete

# CHRISTMAS WEEKEND

### Friday

**SUPPER**

Mushrooms à la Grecque

Sardines en Croûte with Mustard Hollandaise Sauce
Green Salad

Oranges in Caramel

### Saturday

**LUNCH**

Hot Gammon and Cumberland Sauce
Mashed Potatoes
Leeks and Carrots

Crème Brulée

**DINNER**

Eggs in Cream and Herb Sauce

Spiced Leg of Lamb
Julienne of Celery and Potato
Flageolets

Plum Water Ice

### Sunday

**LUNCH**

Boned Turkey with Ham and Chestnut Stuffing
Cranberry Sauce
Roast Potatoes
Brussels Sprouts with Chestnuts

Mincemeat Flan with Brandy Butter

**SUPPER**

Shell Pasta with Ham
Salad

Cheese and Celery

# Friday Supper

## (for 6 people)

### MUSHROOMS A LA GRECQUE

| | |
|---|---|
| 1¼ kg | 2½ lb button mushroom |
| 850 ml | 1½ pints water |
| 150 ml | ¼ pint olive oil |
| 150 ml | ¼ pint lemon juice |
| | ½ teaspoon salt |
| | 6 sprigs parsley, 1 small celery stalk, ¼ teaspoon fennel seeds, ¼ teaspoon thyme, 12 peppercorns and 6 coriander seeds, all tied in a muslin bag |

Place all the ingredients except the mushrooms in a covered saucepan and simmer for 10 minutes. Remove herb bag. Wash and trim the mushrooms, add to the liquid and simmer covered for 10 minutes. Remove mushrooms and boil the liquid rapidly until it has reduced to about ½ pint (275 ml). Check the seasoning and strain the sauce over the mushrooms. Cool and store covered in the fridge.* Before serving sprinkle with parsley or mixed fresh herbs.

PREPARATION TIME 25 minutes.

*Can be made 2 or 3 days in advance.

### SARDINES EN CROUTE WITH MUSTARD HOLLANDAISE SAUCE

| | |
|---|---|
| 2 × 225 g | 2 small packets of frozen puff pastry |
| 3 × 150 g | 3 tins sardines |
| | 3 oz melted butter |
| | Salt and pepper |
| | 2 tablespoons lemon juice |
| | 1 egg yolk |

MUSTARD
HOLLANDAISE SAUCE

| | |
|---|---|
| | 1 large teaspoon French mustard |
| | 1 tablespoon wine vinegar |
| | 3 egg yolks |
| 175 g | 6 oz melted butter |
| | Salt and pepper |

Drain the sardines and mash with a fork in a bowl. Add the melted butter, lemon juice, salt and pepper. Roll out the pastry into two oblongs, pile the sardine mixture on to one and cover with the other, sealing the edges with water. Decorate with left-over pastry and brush with an egg yolk. Bake in a hot oven, 400–450°F 200–°C gas 6–8, for 30 minutes. Serve with a mustard hollandaise sauce.

Another way of preparing the pastry which is very pretty and slightly different is to follow Georgia Langton's recipe for Flamiche in February, page 40.

The sardine mixture and pastry can be prepared separately in advance and assembled at the last moment.

PREPARATION TIME 10 minutes.

Put the vinegar in a saucepan and boil rapidly, reducing by half. Cool and add the egg yolks and mustard. Pour in the hot butter slowly, beating all the time until the mixture thickens. To keep warm place in a bowl over warm water.

### ORANGES IN CARAMEL

175 g  *6 oz granulated sugar*
*2 tablespoons brandy (optional)*
*6 oranges*

Combine the sugar and 2 tablespoons of water in a saucepan and heat gently, stirring until the sugar has melted, then boil hard for 5 minutes until the sugar turns gold (watch carefully). Cool, add brandy and $\frac{1}{4}$ pint (150 ml) water. Leave to cool completely, but do not let it set.

Pare one orange, cutting the peel into thin strips (or use a lemon parer). Blanch, peel, drain and add to the caramel. Skin all the oranges and cut into thin slices, removing pips. Place in a serving dish and pour the cooled caramel sauce over them.

Can be made a day in advance, but no longer, or the oranges may go discoloured.

PREPARATION TIME 12 minutes.

# Saturday Lunch

(for 6 people)

### HOT GAMMON AND CUMBERLAND SAUCE

*4 bay leaves*
*6 peppercorns*
*Water*

CUMBERLAND SAUCE

*Rind of 2 oranges, pared*
*4 tablespoons redcurrant*
  *jelly*
*2 level teaspoons French*
  *mustard*
*8 tablespoons port*
*Pinch of ground ginger*
*Salt and pepper*

LEEKS AND CARROTS

*About 8 even-sized carrots*
  *(not too large)*
*About 6 small leeks*
50 g *2 oz butter*

Use a piece of rolled gammon about 4 lb (2 kg) in weight, if possible with the skin still on.

Boil the gammon in water to cover with the peppercorns and bay leaves for 20 minutes per lb (450 g). When cooked, remove the skin and string, slice and arrange on dish. Pour the Cumberland sauce over the gammon and serve.

If preferred you can leave the joint whole and carve it at the table, in which case skin it after cooking, leaving on as much fat as possible. Score the fat in diamonds, rub with brown sugar, smear with marmalade, push cloves in the centre of each diamond and grill for a few minutes until the sugar has melted. Over the Christmas weekend, however, when there are usually lots of children about, I find it simpler to prepare this in the kitchen.

Pare the oranges and blanch rind in boiling water for 5 minutes. Strain, rinse in cold water. Mix the redcurrant jelly, mustard, ginger, salt and pepper in a bowl, add the orange rinds and put the bowl over hot water, stir until melted. Add the port, stir and cook for a further 5 minutes.

MASHED POTATOES This is a New Zealand recipe using baking powder, and it makes the potatoes lighter.

Boil the potatoes for about 20 minutes in salted water, drain, add 1½ oz (40 g) butter, 2 teaspoons baking powder and mash thoroughly.

Peel and slice carrots thinly and cook for 5 minutes in salted water. Drain. Wash leeks and slice fairly thinly. Put with the carrots and butter in a saucepan, cover and cook gently for another 5 minutes. Add salt and pepper. Drain if there is too much liquid.

### CREME BRULEE

575 ml  *1 pint double cream*
*3 eggs*
50 g  *2 oz sugar*
*1 teaspoon vanilla essence*
*or 1 vanilla pod*
*Demerara sugar*

This must be made a day in advance.

Heat the cream until nearly boiling with the vanilla pod if you are using it. Beat the eggs and sugar together until light, add the vanilla essence if used and slowly pour the cream on to the egg mixture whilst beating. Pour into ovenproof dish and bake at 300°F 150°C gas 2 for ½ hour. Tap the side of the dish gently with fingertips, and if the custard is just beginning to set take it out of the oven. It will continue to cook whilst cooling. Chill well in fridge for 24 hours.

FOR THE TOPPING take custard from the fridge and immediately spread a layer of demerara sugar evenly over the top. Place under a very hot grill until the sugar has melted. Turn to get an even finish. Leave to cool to a hard glaze.

(If using an electric hand whisk) PREPARATION TIME 10 minutes.

# Saturday Dinner
## (for 8 people)

### EGGS IN CREAM AND HERB SAUCE

8 hard-boiled eggs
225 g  8 oz peeled prawns
50 g  2 oz butter
2 tablespoons chopped parsley
2 teaspoons chervil
1½ teaspoons French mustard
Salt and pepper
425 ml  ¾ pint cream
3 tablespoons breadcrumbs
2 tablespoons grated Cheddar

Melt the butter, add the herbs, spices, cream and prawns. Slice the eggs and put in an ovenproof serving dish. Pour the sauce over the eggs, sprinkle with breadcrumbs and grated cheese, and put in a hot oven, 425°F 220°C gas 7, for 10 minutes or until top is golden, or place under a grill for 1–2 minutes and then heat in oven at 350°F 180°C gas 4 for 15 minutes.

PREPARATION TIME 10 minutes.

### SPICED LEG OF LAMB

1¾ kg  1 leg of lamb, about 4 lb
2 tablespoons oil
25 g  1 oz butter
1 large carrot, sliced
1 large onion, sliced
2 sticks celery, sliced
275 ml  ½ pint chicken stock
Bouquet garni
1 teaspoon tomato purée
2 teaspoons flour
  (optional)

MARINADE

2 teaspoons ground
  coriander
1 teaspoon ground cumin
1 teaspoon paprika
1 teaspoon salt
Black pepper
½ teaspoon ground ginger

Mix all the marinade ingredients together. Place the leg of lamb in a basin, rub the spices all over it and leave overnight.*

TO COOK heat the butter and oil in a large ovenproof casserole and brown the leg slowly, taking care not to burn. Remove the lamb, add the vegetables, cover and cook for 5 minutes. Replace the lamb, add the stock, bouquet garni and tomato purée, cover and cook in oven at 325°F 170°C gas 3 for 1½–2 hours or until lamb is tender.

Take out the joint, place it on serving dish and strain the juices. If you prefer a thicker gravy, mix a little of the juice with the flour, stir and add the rest of the juice, boil for 2–3 minutes and pour into a sauce boat.

*Must be marinaded a day in advance.

# Saturday Dinner
## continued

JULIENNE OF CELERY
AND POTATO

|  | |
|---|---|
| | *1 head of celery* |
| | *4 large potatoes* |
| 35 g | *1½ oz butter* |
| | *1 shallot, finely chopped* |
| | *Salt, pepper, parsley* |

FLAGEOLETS

|  | |
|---|---|
| 2 × 270 g | *2 cans flageolets, drained* |
| 25 g | *1 oz butter* |
| | *1 clove garlic, crushed* |
| 270 g | *10 oz can tomatoes* |
| | *Pepper* |

|  | |
|---|---|
| 50 g | *2 oz currants* |
| 100 g | *4 oz raisins* |
| 12 g | *½ oz shredded almonds* |
| 12 g | *½ oz candied peel* |
| 25 g | *1 oz glacé cherries* |
| | *½ wineglass brandy or rum* |
| 175 g | *6 oz block chocolate* |
| | *or* |
| 50 g | *2 oz cocoa and* |
| | *1 tablespoon water* |
| 275 ml | *½ pint single cream* |

ICE CREAM MIXTURE

|  | |
|---|---|
| 275 ml | *½ pint double cream* |
| 50 g | *2 oz granulated sugar* |
| 75 ml | *2½ fluid oz water* |
| | *3 egg yolks* |

DECORATION

|  | |
|---|---|
| 275 ml | *½ pint whipped cream* |
| | *flavoured with brandy* |

Cut the celery and peeled potatoes into julienne strips.*

Heat the butter in a flameproof dish, add shallots and celery, cover and heat for 4–5 minutes, shaking the dish occasionally. Drain the potatoes, dry with a cloth and add to the dish, cover with greaseproof paper and lid. Cook gently for 8 minutes – no longer. Put into a vegetable dish and sprinkle with chopped parsley.

*The potatoes and celery can be prepared the day before and kept in cold water (to prevent discolouration) in the fridge.

Melt the butter and heat with the garlic, pepper and chopped tomatoes. Refresh flageolets with cold water, add to other ingredients and heat through for 5 minutes.

## PLUM WATER ICE

This can be made well in advance and is much more original than a plum pudding. It can be made with either a mousse or a custard.

Wash the currants and raisins well. Chop the almonds and candied peel. Rinse the cherries to get rid of some of the syrup. Pour the brandy or rum over all of these and leave to soak. Dissolve the chocolate in the single cream over a gentle heat. If using cocoa mix with water and cook until boiling, stirring all the time, then add to the single cream. Bring to boiling point, then cool.

TO MAKE AN EGG MOUSSE dissolve the sugar in the water, then boil rapidly without stirring until the mixture reaches the 'thread' stage – 216°–218°F on a sugar thermometer. Remove pan from heat, add the beaten egg yolks and beat until the mixture is mousse-like. Whip double cream lightly and add to the mousse.

AN EASIER WAY IS TO MAKE A CUSTARD beat the egg yolks with the sugar, then add the scalded cream, beating all the time. Cool completely. Whip the double cream and add to the custard mixture.

Combine the chocolate mixture with either the mousse or the custard.

Put in freezer and leave till quite firm, about 2 hours. Remove from freezer, stir in drained fruit, place in a mixing bowl and refreeze.*

One hour before beginning the meal take ice out of the deep freeze, turn out. To turn out, place bowl quickly in hot water and turn on to serving dish. Put a sprig of holly on top of the ice and pipe whipped cream around the bottom. Keep in fridge until wanted.

*Can be prepared in advance.

# Sunday Lunch
(for 6 people)

## BONED TURKEY WITH HAM AND CHESTNUT STUFFING

| | |
|---|---|
| 5 kg | *1 turkey weighing approximately 10 lb boned* |
| 1½ kg | *1 boned collar of bacon or slipper or ham weighing approximately 3 lb* |

STUFFING

| | |
|---|---|
| 1 kg | *2 lb chestnuts, tinned or fresh* |
| | *Liver of turkey, finely chopped* |
| | *4 tablespoons onion, chopped* |
| 100 g | *4 oz butter* |
| 1 kg | *2 lb sausagemeat, pork* |
| | *4 tablespoons fresh breadcrumbs* |
| | *2 eggs* |
| | *1½ teaspoons salt* |
| | *Pepper* |
| | *Big pinch of allspice* |
| | *½ teaspoon thyme* |
| | *2 tablespoons chopped parsley* |
| | *Salt and pepper* |
| | Trussing needle and string, not synthetic. |

The advantage of having turkey cooked like this is that for a large amount of people the carving is very quick. It is also delicious cold. These quantities are for 10 people. If you want to feed fewer people a chicken will do: simply cut down on the quantities for the stuffing. For this weekend I might use ham left over from Saturday's lunch.

Soak the bacon or ham if necessary for two hours to get rid of the excess salt. Boil in water with 6 peppercorns and 2 bay leaves for 20 minutes per lb (450 g). Allow to cool in the liquid. Cut into two equal halves.

Bone the turkey (see page 47) or get your butcher to do it. Drain the chestnuts if tinned. If fresh, peel and boil for 6 minutes. Set aside 8 oz (225 g) to mix with the sprouts, and chop the rest finely. Melt half the butter in a saucepan, add the onions and liver and cook gently for 5 minutes. Mix together the sausagemeat, chopped chestnuts, breadcrumbs, lightly beaten eggs, herbs and spices. Add the liver and onion mixture plus the butter in the pan and mix together – it is easier to do this with your hands.

Lay the boned turkey open on the worktop. Spread with one-third of the stuffing, lay hams in the middle and cover the top and sides with the rest of the stuffing. Bring the sides of the turkey up over stuffing, tucking in excess skin to form a neat parcel. Sew up with string. Turn turkey over and place in a roasting pan.*

Spread with remaining butter, season and roast for 2½ hours at 450°F 230°C gas 8.

It is important for the turkey to rest for at least ½ hour before serving for the stuffing to become easier to handle. Carve across the bird to get slices of breast, stuffing and ham. Use a sharp knife.

TO MAKE GRAVY use the remaining giblets and boil for ½ hour in water with 3 stalks and leaves of parsley, salt and pepper. Strain. Skim fat off the juices in the pan after roasting the turkey, add 2 tablespoons flour and stir slowly, adding stock. Boil for 5 minutes,* strain into a gravy boat. Serve with cranberry sauce.

PREPARATION TIME 30 minutes.

*Can be prepared a day in advance.

BRUSSELS SPROUTS WITH
CHESTNUTS

| | |
|---|---|
| 1 kg | 2 lb Brussels sprouts, trimmed |
| 25 g | 1 oz butter |
| 225 g | 8 oz whole chestnuts |
| | Salt and pepper |

PASTRY

| | |
|---|---|
| 675 g | 1½ lb plain flour |
| 350 g | 12 oz butter |
| | 2 eggs |
| 150 ml | ¼ pint water |

FILLING

3 jars of good quality
  mincemeat
10 tablespoons brandy

BRANDY BUTTER

| | |
|---|---|
| 350 g | 12 oz unsalted butter |
| 350 g | 12 oz icing sugar, or castor sugar for a rougher texture |
| | At least 12 tablespoons brandy |

ROAST POTATOES (3 per person) Scrape potatoes. Cut into even-sized pieces, boil in salted water for 5 minutes. Melt 2 oz (50 g) lard and 1 oz (25 g) butter in a roasting pan, add the strained potatoes, sprinkle with salt and bake in hot oven (whilst roasting turkey), turning occasionally, for about 1 hour.

Boil the water, add salt and Brussels sprouts and cook for 8–10 minutes. Drain, add the butter and chestnuts. Season and mix together lightly.

MINCEMEAT FLAN

Turn mincemeat into a bowl and mix in the brandy. Leave for a few hours or overnight.*
  Make the pastry in a Magimix or by hand (see page 80). Roll two-thirds of the pastry out and line a 10-inch (25-cm) flan dish.* Fill with the mincemeat and roll out the remaining pastry and cover. (I cut a small hole in the middle of the top with a pastry cutter so I can pile brandy butter on top when serving.)
  Cook in oven at 375°F 190°C gas 5 for 35 minutes. Sprinkle with castor sugar. Serve hot with brandy butter, some piled on top at the very last moment, the rest in a bowl.

PREPARATION TIME 12 minutes, having soaked the mincemeat.

*Pastry and mincemeat can be prepared well in advance and assembled at the last minute.

Cream the butter, slowly adding sieved icing sugar, beating all the time. Gradually add the brandy. If the mixture curdles add more icing sugar. Chill. Can be made in Magimix.

PREPARATION TIME 10 minutes.

# Sunday Supper

### SHELL PASTA WITH HAM

Spaghetti or tagliatelle may be used if no shell pasta is available.

225 g  *8 oz pasta shells*
*1 onion, chopped*
25 g  *1 oz butter*
*1 cup chopped ham*
*2 tablespoons chopped*
*parsley*
*Salt and pepper*

Cook the pasta shells in boiling salted water for 6 minutes. Add some cold water to prevent the pasta from sticking and then drain. Soften the onion and add with the ham, parsley, salt and pepper to the pasta shells. Mix all together and serve with a mixed salad.

Cheese and celery to follow.

# Caroline Hulse

---

**Friday**

SUPPER

Mushroom and Celery Salad with a Red Wine Sauce

Minced Pork Cutlets with Tomato Sauce
Fried Potatoes
White Cabbage

Apple Pudding

**Saturday**

LUNCH

Celeriac in Mustard Mayonnaise

Frankfurter Soup with Hot French Bread
Cheese

DINNER

Curried Prawns

Loin of Lamb with a Wine and Herb Sauce
Potatoes cooked with Oranges
Peas and Cucumber cooked in Butter and Mint

Lemon Ice and Almond Biscuits

**Sunday**

LUNCH

Beef Stew
Mashed Potatoes
Brussels Sprouts

Apricot and Ginger Roll with Whipped Cream

SUPPER

Eggs in Snow

---

# Friday Supper

(for 6 people)

## MUSHROOM AND CELERY SALAD WITH A RED WINE SAUCE

225 g   *8 oz button mushrooms*
*4 rashers bacon, rinded
   and cut in squares*
*1 large red or green pepper*
*3 sticks celery*
*1 glass red wine*
*2 tablespoons oil*
*1 tablespoon parsley,
   chopped*
*1 clove garlic, crushed*

**VINAIGRETTE**

*3 tablespoons olive oil*
*½ tablespoon tarragon
   vinegar*
*Salt and pepper*

Wash and slice the mushrooms, then sauté them in oil for 1 minute, add the garlic and bacon and cook for a few minutes. Add the wine, boil for 1 minute, then simmer for 5 more minutes. Stir in the chopped parsley. Cool.

Slice the pepper and celery finely and toss them in the vinaigrette. Put the mixture into a serving bowl and pile the mushroom mixture on top.*

PREPARATION TIME 30 minutes.

*This can be made in the morning and put in a cool place, covered in cling film.

## MINCED PORK CUTLETS

These are very cheap to make and children love them.

750 g   *1½ lb minced pork*
*6 tablespoons breadcrumbs*
150 g   *5 oz butter*
*3 eggs*
*3 lemons*
275 ml   *½ pint cream*
*Paprika*
*Parsley*
*2 tablespoons tomato
   ketchup*
*Worcester sauce*
*1 small glass white wine*
*Salt and pepper*

Season the minced pork, add 3 oz (75 g) butter, breadcrumbs and eggs and a dash of Worcester sauce. Mix well together (I put mine in the Magimix) shape the mixture into cutlets – make a ball and then flatten it out, making a tail at the end.* Melt the rest of the butter in a frying pan and fry the cutlets gently till well done, about 10 minutes on each side. Remove and keep warm.

Pour off the surplus butter but keep the scrapings, add the wine and reduce a little over a gentle heat. Add the cream, tomato ketchup and a dash of Worcester sauce. Pour over the meat, dust with a little paprika and decorate with wedges of lemon and chopped parsley.

*The cutlets can be prepared in advance – they take 15 minutes. The cooking and sauce take very little time to prepare at the last minute.

Serve with fried or mashed potatoes, and shredded white cabbage fried for a few minutes in butter (see page 27).

### APPLE PUDDING

1 kg    *2 lb cooking apples*
      *5 tablespoons water*
85 g   *3½ oz sugar*
      *Pinch of cinnamon*
      *3 eggs*

      CARAMEL

75 g   *3 oz sugar*
      *3 tablespoons water*

Oil a 1½-pint (850-ml) ring mould using olive oil if possible.

CARAMEL Dissolve the sugar in the water by heating it slowly in a saucepan, boil, then reduce the heat until the mixture just bubbles. Keep watching and remove from the heat when it has turned a deep amber. Do not burn. Pour in 1 tablespoon of water, stirring until thoroughly blended. Pour the caramel immediately into the mould, swirl it round to coat all the sides (use a brush to help) cool and re-oil any parts of the mould which have not been caramelized.

Peel, quarter, core and slice the apples. Cook in water over a high heat until just cooked – almost a purée. Stir in the sugar and cinnamon, sieve or liquidize and beat in the eggs. When cool, pour into the mould and poach in a *bain marie* for 1 hour in a moderate oven, 350°F 180°C gas 4. Cool till tepid, unmould, but leave the mould on top. Cool in the fridge.* Just before serving fill the centre with whipped cream.

PREPARATION TIME 30 minutes.

*Can be prepared in advance.

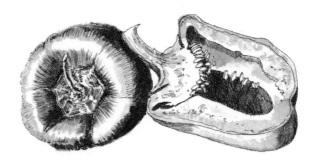

# Saturday Lunch

## (for 6 people)

### CELERIAC IN MUSTARD MAYONNAISE

2 celeriac
1 rounded tablespoon
    chopped chives or parsley
½ pint mayonnaise
    (see page 116)
1 tablespoon French mustard
2 lemons
Salt and pepper

Peel the uncooked celeriac and chop into thick matchsticks (I do mine in the Mouli) and put into a mixture of lemon juice and water so it does not discolour.* Drain and mix with the mayonnaise to which you have added the mustard. Pile on to a serving dish and sprinkle over with the chives or parsley.

PREPARATION TIME 15 minutes.

*Can be prepared a day in advance and assembled at the last minute.

### FRANKFURTER SOUP

150 ml  2 pints stock (preferably
            home-made chicken)
        2 medium potatoes, peeled
            and diced
        4 medium leeks
225 g   8 oz turnips
225 g   8 oz carrots
        1 celery stalk
100 g   4 oz streaky bacon in one
            piece or thick rashers,
            rinded and chopped
        4 frankfurters
        Salt and pepper

Bring the stock and potatoes to the boil, cover and simmer until the potatoes are soft, about 10 minutes. Liquidize. Trim the leeks, split, cut into ¼-inch (6-mm) slices and wash well. Peel and dice the root vegetables and cut the celery into small dice. Fry the chopped bacon in its own fat very slowly until crisp. Return the potatoes to the saucepan together with the prepared vegetables and bacon, bring to simmering point, cover and cook gently for 1 hour.* Thinly slice the frankfurters and just before serving stir them into the soup and heat through.

PREPARATION AND COOKING TIME 1¾ hours.

*This can be prepared the day before.

Serve with hot French bread and butter.

Follow with a good English cheese, blue Cheshire if possible, and bread.

# Saturday Dinner

## (for 8 people)

### CURRIED PRAWNS

500 g 　*1 lb peeled prawns, frozen*
　　　　*or fresh*
　　　*2 small onions, thinly sliced*
　　　*12 tomatoes*
　　　*Juice of 1 lemon*
125 g 　*4 oz butter*
　　　*2 tablespoons curry powder,*
　　　　*to taste*
　　　*Salt*
　　　*4 tablespoons cream, to taste*

This is delicious cold or hot. If serving hot I would cook rice to go with it.

Marks and Spencers do very good frozen prawns; and when tomatoes are expensive you could use half fresh and half tinned.

Fry the onions in the butter until light golden, then stir in the curry powder and a seasoning of salt. Add the peeled and quartered tomatoes and a little water and simmer until the tomatoes are cooked. Purée and rub through a sieve. Cook the purée to reduce it to the right thickness and add the lemon juice and cream to taste. Add the prawns and heat through. Keep warm.

### LOIN OF LAMB WITH A WINE AND HERB SAUCE

2 kg 　*1 loin of lamb, about 4½ lb.*
　　　　*Get your butcher*
　　　　*to chine it*
　　　*½ nutmeg*
　　　*2 teaspoons dried sage*
　　　*1 teaspoon dried marjoram*
　　　*4 tablespoons lamb's fat*
　　　　*or dripping*
　　　*2 cloves garlic, crushed*
　　　*5 tablespoons freshly*
　　　　*chopped parsley*
575 ml 　*1 pint red wine*
　　　*1 tablespoon butter*
　　　*1 tablespoon flour*
　　　*Salt and pepper*

Pre-heat the oven to 350°F 180°C gas 4. Rub the meat all over with salt and freshly ground black pepper and nutmeg, the sage and marjoram. Melt the fat in a roasting dish and brown the meat all over. Pour in the wine, garlic and parsley and cook the meat uncovered in the oven for ½ hour, turning the meat occasionally. Remove the meat and keep warm. Put the roasting pan with the fat back on top of the stove and bring to simmering point. Work the butter and flour together to a paste, add to the fat and mix well (with a balloon mixer if you have one). Return to simmering point again, by which time it will have thickened. Season and pour into a warmed jug.

PREPARATION TIME 5 minutes　COOKING TIME 45 minutes.

# Saturday Dinner

continued

### POTATOES COOKED WITH ORANGES

500 g   *1 lb potatoes*
*2 small oranges*
*4 shallots or 1 medium onion*
*Salt and pepper*
25 g   *1 oz butter*
*2 tablespoons cream if required*
*½ teaspoon sugar*
*1 beaten egg*

Boil the unpeeled oranges in water for 30 minutes. Peel and boil the potatoes until cooked. Mash the potatoes very well. Chop the shallots finely and soften them in butter without colouring them. Cut the oranges into thin slices and remove the pips. Chop them finely and add to the shallots with the salt, pepper and sugar. Cook slowly for another 8 minutes. Add the orange mixture to the potatoes, add the cream and a little butter if necessary to make a firm purée. (I put it all in the Magimix.)

Take a generous teaspoon of the mixture and roll it into a ball, or fill a 2-inch (5-cm) round pastry cutter. Put the potato cakes into a greased ovenproof dish, allowing them space to spread a little.* Brush each cake with a little beaten egg and bake in a hot oven, 450°F 230°C gas 8, for about 12 minutes.

*The mixture can be made well in advance and the cakes cooked while you are eating your first course.

### PEAS AND CUCUMBER COOKED IN BUTTER AND MINT

750 g   *1½ lb frozen petit pois*
*1 cucumber*
50 g   *2 oz butter*
*Sprig of mint*
*1 teaspoon sugar*
*Salt and pepper*

Peel the cucumber, cut into 1-inch (3-cm) slices and then into thick matchsticks, sprinkle with salt and leave to drain. Melt the butter in a saucepan, add the drained and dried cucumber and cook gently with the lid on for 3 minutes, stirring the pan occasionally. Put in the defrosted peas, mint, sugar and seasoning, cover and stew gently for a further 5 minutes.

These will keep in warmer for at least ½ hour.

# *Saturday Dinner*

## continued

### LEMON ICE

4 lemons
175 g   *6 oz icing sugar*
200 ml   *⅓ pint double cream*
275 ml   *½ pint water*

Peel the lemons very thinly. Squeeze the juice. Put the lemon skins in a saucepan with the water and sugar and simmer for 20 minutes. Cool; strain and add to the lemon juice. Leave till cold.

Lightly whip the cream and, stirring gently, add the lemon juice, mix until smooth, pour into a box and freeze for 2½–3 hours, taking it out and stirring it twice during that time.

This can be made days in advance.

Serve with almond biscuits.

### ALMOND BISCUITS

50 g   *2 oz butter*
75 g   *3 oz castor sugar*
37 g   *1½ oz whole wheat or plain flour*
37 g   *1½ oz finely chopped almonds*
    *2 egg whites*

Cream the butter and sugar until very soft. Add the flour, almonds and stiffly beaten egg whites. Place teaspoonfuls of the mixture on well oiled baking sheets and spread thinly. Bake in the centre of oven at 380°F 190°C gas 5 for 6–8 minutes. Remove, cool on a wire rack and store in an airtight container.

These keep for at least 10 days.

# Sunday Lunch

(for 6 people)

---

### BEEF STEW

| | |
|---|---|
| 1 kg | *2 lb topside of beef* |
| 125 g | *4 oz salt pork or unsmoked streaky bacon* |
| | *1 large onion* |
| | *1 teaspoon thyme, chopped* |
| | *1 tablespoon parsley, chopped* |
| | *2 bay leaves* |
| 150 ml | *¼ pint red wine* |
| | *2 tablespoons olive oil* |
| 275 ml | *½ pint meat stock, veal if possible* |
| | *1 clove garlic, crushed* |
| | *1 tablespoon flour* |
| | *1 bouquet garni of thyme, parsley and bay leaf* |
| | *1 tablespoon dripping* |
| 25 g | *1 oz butter* |
| 225 g | *8 oz small button mushrooms, washed* |
| | *12 small shallots* |
| | *Salt and pepper* |

Cut the beef into slices about 2½ inches (6 cm) square and ¼ inch (6 mm) thick. Put into a bowl, season with salt and pepper, cover with the sliced onion, herbs, olive oil and red wine and leave to marinade for 3–6 hours.

Cut the bacon into ¼-inch (6-mm) matchsticks. In a casserole (about 4 pint – 2 litre – capacity) melt the dripping and add the bacon strips. Add the whole peeled shallots and let them brown, turning frequently, over a low heat. Remove the bacon when nicely browned. Set aside.

Keeping the marinade, drain and dry the meat and add it to the fat, sprinkle on the flour and shake the pan so the flour mixes with the fat. Strain the marinade and pour it into the pan; cook, bubbling for a minute, add the stock, garlic and bouquet garni, cover the casserole and simmer for 2 hours on top of the stove.*

Just before serving cook the mushrooms for a minute or two, to rid them of some of their moisture, and add them to the casserole with the bacon and onions. Heat through.

*This can be made well in advance. Reheat in a medium oven until bubbling – about ½ hour, then add the bacon, mushrooms and onions.

Serve with mashed potatoes and Brussels sprouts cooked for about 6 minutes in boiling salted water.

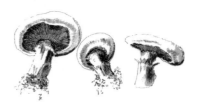

### APRICOT AND GINGER ROLL

125 g    *4 oz dried apricots*
*1 cooking apple*

**CAKE MIX**

150 g    *5 oz plain flour*
*½ teaspoon each mixed spice,*
     *cinnamon and ground ginger*
125 g    *4 oz golden syrup and black*
     *treacle mixed*
75 g    *Scant 3 oz butter*
*1 large egg*
125 ml    *4 fluid oz warm water*
*1 teaspoon bicarbonate*
     *of soda*
*Castor sugar*

Soak the apricots for 3 hours, then purée. Cook and purée the apple and add to the apricots.

Prepare a paper case for a Swiss roll (see page 85) or brush a baking tin, about 8 inches (20 cm) by 10 inches (25 cm), well with oil. Dredge a sheet of greaseproof paper with castor sugar.

Sift the flour and spices together and warm the treacle with the butter. Be careful not to let it get too hot. Beat the egg and add to the syrup mixture with the water and the soda, pour in flour, spices and beat well for about 10 seconds. Turn on to the prepared case and bake in a moderate oven, 350°F 180°C gas 4, for 7–8 minutes or until firm to touch.

Turn out the cake on to the greaseproof paper, trim the edges and spread with the fruit purée. Roll up from the long side like a Swiss roll, tip on to a serving dish, dredge with castor sugar and serve with cream.

PREPARATION TIME 15 minutes, but remember to soak the apricots 3 hours in advance.

## Sunday Supper

### (for 2 people)

### EGGS IN SNOW

*2 large eggs*
*2 tablespoons double cream*
*2 tablespoons grated*
     *Parmesan*
*Salt and white pepper*

Butter 2 large ramekins or individual casserole dishes with butter. Separate the eggs and beat the whites very stiffly, season well with salt and pepper and divide them equally into the dishes. Make a depression with the back of a spoon in the centre of the whites and place one yolk carefully in each hollow. Cover each egg with a tablespoon of cream and a tablespoon of cheese. Bake in a hot oven, 450°F 230°C gas 8, for about 8 minutes.

Serve immediately with hot bread and butter.

# INDEX